Praise for *Let Your*

"This book is going to be a valuable tool for people who are serious about their spiritual journey. It's one of those topics that people can't get enough of and I want to thank Debra for taking on a huge topic in such a beautiful way."

—ECHO BODINE, author of
My Big Book of Healing and *Echoes of the Soul*

"It may sound contradictory, but Debra Engle is an inspirational writer with a down-to-earth style. Her conversational tone has a way of putting us at ease. Her personal anecdotes make it undeniable that we all have the ability to enter into relationship with our spirit guides. In *Let Your Spirit Guides Speak*, she encourages and nurtures us until we relax into the possibility that our spirit guides are not fantasies or distant mysteries, but are literally by our side whenever we are ready to request their help. By the end of this page turner, nothing feels more pressing than tuning in to those forces that are only here to uplift and love us."

—AMY TORRES, author of
Sweet Dreams of Awakening

"If you want to learn ways to connect with your spirit guides, Debra Engle has provided the map to do so. She outlines ways to do so, accompanied by stories and examples that illustrate these ways. *Let Your Spirit Guides Speak* is a must have for spiritual seekers!"

—DR. STEVEN FARMER, international author,
spiritual psychotherapist, and shamanic healer

"Let Your Spirit Guides Speak is a masterful work for realizing your inner mystic—the absolute guide to finding purpose, peace, and joy."

—MAYA TIWARI, Ayurveda pioneer,
spiritual teacher, and author

Praise for *The Only Little Prayer You Need*

"A delightful little book on healing our fear-based thoughts through prayer."

—JON MUNDY, PhD, author of
Living A Course in Miracles
and publisher of *Miracles* magazine

"Debra Engle's *The Only Little Prayer You Need* took my breath away as I sat reading it. Like Engle, I, too, have been a student of *A Course in Miracles* for thirty years. And also like her, it has taught me all the important spiritual tools I rely on every day. However, her little prayer provides a much-needed shortcut to peace-filled living that everyone, Course student or not, can use daily. Hourly, even minute by minute. Thank you, Debra. I needed to read your book today. I needed to shift my perception on a current situation and your book and prayer did just that for me."

—KAREN CASEY, PhD, author of
Each Day a New Beginning

LET YOUR
SPIRIT GUIDES
SPEAK

LET YOUR
SPIRIT GUIDES
SPEAK

A Simple Guide
for a Life of Purpose,
Abundance, and Joy

DEBRA LANDWEHR ENGLE

HAMPTON ROADS

Cover design by Jim Warner
Cover art © Peter Zelei/iStock
Interior designed by Kathryn Sky-Peck

Hampton Roads Publishing Company, Inc.
Charlottesville, VA 22906
Distributed by Red Wheel/Weiser, LLC
www.redwheelweiser.com

Sign up for our newsletter and special offers by going to www.redwheelweiser.com/newsletter/

ISBN: 978-1-57174-740-2

Library of Congress Cataloging-in-Publication Data

Names: Engle, Debra Landwehr, author.
Title: Let your spirit guides speak : a simple guide for a life of purpose,
   abundance, and joy / Debra Landwehr Engle.
Description: Charlottesville : Hampton Roads Pub., 2016.
Identifiers: LCCN 2016008013 | ISBN 9781571747402 (5 x 7 tp : alk. paper)
Subjects: LCSH: Guides (Spiritualism)
Classification: LCC BF1275.G85 E54 2016 | DDC 133.9--dc23
LC record available at http://lccn.loc.gov/2016008013

Printed in the United States of America
MG
10 9 8 7 6 5 4 3 2

Contents

Introduction

A FEW MONTHS AGO, I sat at a bagel shop having lunch with a friend. We talked, as we always do, about the ups and downs of our lives: her challenges as a single mom, what it takes to run a business, how much we love lemon bars.

One of the things I treasure about our conversations is that, underneath them all, there's a spiritual thread. Our discussions are not so much about what we've done, but what it all *means*. Even when we're raving about lemon bars, we're *really* talking about abundance and joy (which, to be fair, may then be followed up with a conversation that's *really* about losing weight).

During this particular conversation, I mentioned something I find myself talking about more and more these days: my spirit guides. I told her that I'd spent time listening to them that morning, and they'd given me another *aha* insight.

My friend looked at me and began to cry.

"What's wrong?" I asked.

"I forget," she said. "I forget that we have guides. I forget that I'm never alone."

It was poignant to see this powerhouse of a young woman brought to tears by the reminder of spiritual comfort—something we all have and constantly forget.

That's why I'm writing this book.

I've been blessed to be aware of spirit guides—or angels, light beings, or entities by other names—as a constant and real presence in my life since my youth. But it's only recently that I've been brave enough to talk about them out loud.

Clearly, my guides think it's time.

When I wrote *The Only Little Prayer You Need*, I alluded to the idea that we're moving into a new conversation with Spirit. We need to go beyond prayer to build a co-creative relationship—a relationship in which not only do our guides help us fulfill *our* purpose, but we help extend *their* love into this world. We work not just for our own good, but for the good of the whole.

And judging by the fear-driven conflict and acrimony we're bombarded with daily, that's going to take some intervention.

I'm writing this book because we have a vast resource of spiritual help available to us, and we're not making the best

"

*This is a gift
that all of us on the
planet right now
have been given.*

"

use of it. We feel cut off from it, we're afraid of it, we think we're not worthy, or we snort in a cynical sort of way when someone mentions the possibility that spiritual guidance exists. After all, aside from 84 percent of the world's population, who would actually believe in a spiritual power?

The point is that there are unseen helpers for all of us. Instead of waiting for them to get our attention or prove they exist, we need to throw up the veil between our worlds and say, "I want to know you. I want to hear you. I want to work with you."

This is a gift that all of us on the planet right now have been given. We have the opportunity to explore and understand personal spiritual guidance in a way that few people have been able to before. We can take spiritual texts seriously when they talk about angels and guides. And we get to fully embrace this remarkable time, when even quantum physics acknowledges other planes of existence.

Think about it this way: Imagine you're an astronaut, and the group in the control room at NASA is your team of spirit guides. They can't control every decision you make. But they are with you constantly, watching everything you do, and they are available every moment if you have a question or need help.

Like the team at NASA, our guides accompany us on our journey. They nudge, advise, protect, and companion us. And, if we listen, they help ensure that we complete our Earth mission with the greatest success.

MANY YEARS AGO, author Gary Zukav appeared on *Oprah* discussing soul growth. When they opened up the discussion to questions from the audience, a woman asked Zukav if she should start her own jewelry business.

"Why," he said, "are you asking me?"

His response woke me up to a major problem in my life, which I believe is a major problem in all our lives: we keep looking to other people for answers, which may give us a quick fix but eventually leaves us disappointed, frustrated, and seeking once again.

Our politicians don't have our answers, nor do our religious leaders, our teachers, our coaches, or our counselors. The best they can do, just like the rest of us, is advise and counsel based on what they've learned and believe. This can be useful, but it's always limited by our own experience, and often shadowed by fear.

So, if that's the problem, what's the solution?

Turning inward and asking for the guidance that's designed specifically for you.

This is the point where your ego will flare up and say, *Uh-uh. Not going there. Let's go get a hot fudge sundae.* It does this because its

"

And, if we listen, they help ensure that we complete our Earth mission with the greatest success.

"

entire identity depends on fear, which is why, in the words of *A Course in Miracles*, it keeps seeking and not finding.

It keeps not finding success, love, joy, growth, well-being, peace of mind—or at least not for very long. And then it turns to another outside expert for a roadmap instead of looking to the only voice that can help without bias or limitations: Spirit. Inner guidance. God. Your personal GPS.

Now, believe me, I know that going within can seem frightening at first. For instance: What if you're having marital problems and you're afraid your guides will tell you that it's all your fault?

What if your child is dealing with addiction and you blame yourself as a parent?

What if you're on the edge financially and your guidance tells you that you'll never get out of the hole you're in?

These are ego questions, designed to keep you from introducing yourself to your spiritual guidance. How do I know? Because they're all based on fear and self-judgment. And the one thing your guides will never do is judge you. Ever.

They will honor every decision you've ever made for the growth and courage it required. And then they'll help you make decisions that serve you better and more effortlessly from that point on—not just once in a while, but day after day. Every time you show up, they'll be there, ready to solve that one problem of looking for external answers (and not finding them) once and for all.

Because that one problem comes from the core belief that we're somehow separate from a higher power.

And the one solution is to remember that we can never be separate from that power.

How better to learn that—to be reminded every single day—than to communicate directly with Spirit, feeling the comforting embrace and gentle guidance of those who know us best?

WHENEVER I SIT DOWN and start a conversation with my guides, they answer me by saying, "We are here with you always." It's their signature. And then the conversation begins. Some days the information seems mundane. Other days they open up a new path in my thinking that I didn't know existed. But, always, they remind me that I'm more than my body, my address, my work, my marriage, and my lemon bars.

Let Your Spirit Guides Speak is a book about what it means to live a life that's divinely guided by direct experience with Spirit. In this book, I'll share what I've learned about developing a collaborative relationship with guidance and the practical steps you can take to deepen your connection into a conscious, co-creative conversation.

Throughout the book, I'm going to use the words God, Holy Spirit, spiritual guides, angels, and other terms liberally. If any of them gets in your way, please feel free to replace them with words that make sense to you. I'm writing this from my own life and with the generous sharing of experiences from other people I know. I'm not writing it out of a particular theology. Your relationship with Spirit is personal, founded on your own beliefs and background.

You may discover specific entities on your team. Or you may find that your guidance arrives as a less-defined energy or knowing. What matters is the message, comfort, and knowledge you receive.

You may find your relationship with Spirit entering into a whole new realm—beyond individual desire, beyond asking for forgiveness or grace, beyond being imprisoned by fear. This relationship does, in fact, take us even beyond prayer itself to a new conversation that is as real as the one you and I are having right now.

That's why I'm also including messages just the way they showed up for me in writing this book. Early in the process, I sat at the computer with my hands on the keyboard and my eyes closed, as I often do, waiting for direction. One particular day, I saw the face of a woman I hadn't met, although she was entirely familiar. I realized that she could be the composite of a hundred women I know: wise, intelligent, gentle, and compassionate, yet with a glint of mischievousness.

When I asked who she was, I heard, "She's your writing guide. She will help you expressly in writing and completing this book."

Aha. My writing buddy. A guide who knows exactly what this book needs to include and how to present it. I call her Ella, and ever since I met her, I've started each period of writing with a short chat with her, my hands poised over the keyboard. Typically, those chats have led directly into the topic for the day, most of which have taken me by complete surprise.

You'll find her messages in a different font introduced by a leaf image throughout this book. I've chosen not to paraphrase them, but to present them in their entirety because they carry an energy and clarity that would be lost if I tried to restate them. Plus, they'll show you the kinds of messages that are available to you as you partner with Spirit in your own unique way.

It's easy to get overwhelmed by the enormity of the problems we face in our daily lives and on the planet: climate change, depletion of resources, poverty, oppression, violence.

But think of what's possible if we work with Spirit and ask for creative solutions, for downloads of information, for new ways of approaching these challenges without fear.

Our spirit guides, just like Jesus, Gandhi, Martin Luther King, Jr., and other leaders whose voices endure through the ages, challenge us to live from our better nature. To make decisions from love rather than fear. To live from our higher Self rather than our ego. To know that it's possible to practice non-violence, to listen rather than to jump to conclusions, and to understand that every conflict, whether it's between countries or in our own mind, is a civil war.

If we can remember the unlimited spiritual guidance available to us, our problems—even the global ones—pale in comparison. Nothing is more powerful than the healing love of these spirit helpers. And when we draw on their assistance, we accelerate and amplify what's possible for us and those around us.

There is no problem we cannot solve. But we need to ask for help from Spirit constantly—not just when we're in crisis or we happen to remember. That means developing an ongoing relationship that's different from how we might have thought of it before.

As my friend at the bagel shop expressed, it's easy to feel very alone in this world. Even in a crowd, even if you're

"

Nothing is more powerful than the healing love of these spirit helpers.

"

successful by the world's standards, even in a marriage, even in a friendly neighborhood or busy workplace, we can feel adrift and far from home, and all our fears start chewing on us and eating us away, nibble by nibble.

This makes life a struggle that it doesn't need to be. And it prevents us from fully giving and receiving in life, limiting our ability to realize our own potential.

So, listen to what I'm telling you, even if you think it's a little far-fetched at first:

You have helpers standing right next to you. Introduce yourself. Ask them to introduce themselves to you. Close your eyes and let yourself feel their presence. Thank them even though you don't know them yet.

Say yes. Be willing. And above all, believe that their help is as present and steadfast as the beating of your own heart.

Claiming Your Inner Mystic

I consider myself a mystic who makes mushroom soup casseroles. My pantry is full of those cream soups that are staples of midwestern kitchens and Thanksgiving tables. But while I'm stirring up a base for a green bean casserole, I'm likely to have a conversation in my mind. Not with myself, but with my spirit guides.

A few years ago, it was about my husband Bob's aunt. She was looking for a part to fit an old woodburning stove and didn't know where to shop for it. I was loading the dishwasher after supper one night, and suddenly I heard the word "Sears" plain as day.

I yelled into the next room to Bob: "The guides say she can get it at Sears."

Sure enough, Sears was the one store that had it.

Some people might chalk this up to intuition, psychic abilities, or a good guess. But I credit my guides, those unseen helpers who float answers into my mind as though they were messages in a bottle bobbing along my stream of consciousness.

It may seem like a waste asking guides about replacement parts. Shouldn't their guidance be focused on something grander and more sacred? That's one of many things I've learned about my guides. As much as we expect them to be beings of light, concerned only with soul growth, they're a lot like your best friend walking beside you. Whatever you're interested in and whatever could help you is of equal importance to them.

MY DAD TAUGHT ME that we're surrounded by guidance from the spiritual realms. In the dance of all our relationships, we have many partners we cannot see. I don't know that he expected to teach me this; I don't even know that he taught it to me directly. It was my mom, after all, who read *Autobiography of a Yogi* and another book with the word "clairvoyant" in the title, which stumped me as a young reader.

I don't remember my dad talking about spirits or guides, but he and my mom subscribed to the *UFO* and *FATE* magazines that sat on the end tables in our basement recreation room, where I would curl up on the sofa on hot summer days and read stories of people who remembered lives in different bodies and different times, or people who'd had near-death experiences, touching the other side and coming back to report it. Even when our family sat around the supper table, eating meatloaf and cornbread, I had a sense that my dad knew things that he wasn't talking about.

This was an extraordinary world, this blend of metaphysics and the supernatural with my family's German heritage, which included an appreciation for the land and the people for whom the term "salt of the earth" could have been coined. My dad was fifty-two years old when I, the youngest of six children, was born. My early memories are of taking him to the train station and airport for his travels as a government auditor. He had his first major heart attack when I was eleven, and it seemed he was in the hospital for months. I suppose I was always afraid of him leaving one way or another, so when he was home, sitting at the head of the table or calling me Debbie Debbie, he wasn't the one I went to for counsel or advice.

Yet even from an emotional distance, he helped set me on two paths in my adult life, no matter how much I denied them in my younger years. One was the path back to the land, to gardening, to the sacred connection of putting your hands in

"

I believe in direct communication with God. When we are part of the Divine, how could it be otherwise?

"

the dirt. The other was the path of spiritual awakening, of skipping over accepted religious tenets and daring to live the life of a mystic. In this, he modeled what I have come to know as our purpose for being: to plant our feet firmly on the earth while we call forth the loving kindness of heaven.

I believe in direct communication with God. When we are part of the Divine, how could it be otherwise?

SEVERAL YEARS AGO, I visited my mom in the house where I grew up. She had just celebrated her eighty-ninth birthday, and she was picking up a wheelbarrow full of sticks, cleaning the yard for the coming spring. I sat in my brother's old bedroom, still painted yellow, with a plastic flower arrangement on the wall near the desk that my mom had antiqued in the 1970s. I began looking at the shelves in his room, which held these books: the Bible, *Family Safety and First Aid*, *Birds of North America*, and Garrison Keillor's *Leaving Home*. My mom's 1939 copy of *Gone with the Wind* with the binding falling apart sat on those shelves, along with her stash of magazines that included stories I'd written.

Most of the books, though, were mystical in nature: *Cosmic Consciousness*, *The Autobiography of a Medium*, *Exploring the Psychic World*, *Quantum Healing*, *The Unity Way of Life*, *Strange Prophecies that*

Came True, The Principles of Theosophy, Between Two Worlds, and five books on American mystic Edgar Cayce.

Among them was *Autobiography of a Yogi,* which my mom credited with rescuing her from a deep depression in the 1950s. My dad's brother Marvin was visiting at the time. They were talking about spiritual realms, and my mom opened the linen closet and found the book right in front. She hadn't seen it before and never learned how it got there.

As I think back, I realize that, as children, we had a smorgasbord of thought from which to choose. Family bookshelves held classic literature, books on nature, Bible stories, Bobbsey Twins and Hardy Boys, fishing, home repair, history, anthropology, math, and science. We were free to select those ideas that spoke to us, to read the books that called our name.

It's no surprise, then, that six children could be closely tied yet individual in their expressions of life. Each of us was touched in some way by the birds and the gardening as well as the more esoteric realms. We could accept or reject the ideas not out of judgment, but based on whether they reflected part of who we were and strengthened our core belief system.

This, I think, is a model for how we can exist in this world, particularly with the help of our spiritual guidance: to recognize that each of us was born with a different purpose to fulfill, and that we will gravitate toward the information and ideas that

"

I believe

mystical experiences

can happen

anywhere and

any time.

"

support us. This is freedom. This is acknowledgement of the soul. This is what our guides are here to help us learn.

For centuries, having conversations with light beings was reserved for priests and monastics. But no longer.

I didn't have special training to talk to my guides. They just showed up. Actually, I'm pretty sure they're showing up for all of us every single moment of our lives and have been from before we were born. But because we don't have our radios tuned to them—and often don't even know there *is* a radio—we miss out on an enormous life support system that could make our lives infinitely easier and more enjoyable.

Mysticism has been defined as a direct union with or experience of God, an understanding that we are one with the Divine and can receive direct communication, without the need for an intercessor or priest.

The list of people who considered themselves mystics might surprise you. Florence Nightingale, known as the mother of modern nursing, wrote: "Where shall I find God? In myself. That is the true Mystical Doctrine."

And Albert Einstein, theoretical physicist, said, "The most beautiful emotion we can experience is the mystical. It is the power of all true art and science."

But mysticism is not reserved just for the most advanced thinkers, contemplatives, or those who are closest to the earth.

It is a part of life—as natural as breathing. Being part of God, the only thing *unnatural* is to forget our connection to the Divine, and to operate as though we're adrift, which is what our fears do to us every day.

That's why it's important to bring mysticism into our everyday experiences, out of the realm of monastery walls and special rituals and into our houses and daily routines, as common as fixing a meal or loading the dishwasher.

I believe mystical experiences can happen anywhere and any time: when we're driving to the grocery store, taking out the trash, sitting in a meeting, even putting fried onion rings on top of a green bean casserole.

The only thing required to be mystics in this everyday world is willingness. A willingness to listen more deeply, to be quiet for a few minutes each day, to suspend judgment, and to enter into the relationship with acceptance and a literally open mind.

Are you qualified to have a relationship with your guides? You may think the answer is no. You may believe that you're not worthy, not good enough, or not spiritual or religious enough. You may think you don't deserve it, as though guides pick and choose, selecting only those who pass a cosmic test. They don't.

"

They are Love,

they are with you,

and you can trust them.

"

From what I've seen and understand to be true, the question is not *whether* you deserve to have a relationship. The only question is *when* will you start building one?

I believe that all of us have unseen helpers who are with us constantly. I know this begs all sorts of questions. Are they God? Jesus? The Holy Spirit? Are they loved ones who are on the other side? Are they people we've known before?

Here's what I can tell you from my own experience: They are beings who extend the love of the Creator but are with us always in a close and eminently practical relationship. They have been with us since before we were born, helping us make decisions about this lifetime, and they accompany us along the way.

Guides can take many forms. People have told me about a wide range of types, including a Native American grandmother, a gender-neutral being named Francis (or Frances), angels, an owl totem animal, a straight-talking creole woman from New Orleans, and entities with such high vibrations that they have no defined shape or personality. Through my stepdaughter, we've become acquainted with a Native American who frequents our house and serves as a spirit guide for our property.

Guides are messengers of light. Many have experienced their own lifetimes in physical bodies and are well aware of the challenges of being human. And, ultimately, guides are always representatives of love. While I believe that dark energies or lower-vibration entities exist out of fear, they don't serve as guides. In fact, our guides can help protect us from their intrusions.

It's important to let any preconceptions about your guides fall away, and not to get caught up in any expectations of who they might or should be.

They are Love, they are with you, and you can trust them.

Engaging in Spirit envy, as in "How come she can see her guides and I can't?" and "Why don't I have an archangel as my guide?" is simply the ego talking and has nothing to do with real communication.

So how can you build a relationship with your guidance? Let's assume you've been using *The Only Little Prayer You Need*, which means you've been asking the Holy Spirit to heal your fear-based thoughts about everything. This prayer opens the door to a new conversation with your guides in several important ways:

- You're approaching Spirit not from a standpoint of being broken or sinful, but as a child of God. This implies a relationship in which you're valued from the start. You do not need to establish your worth to yourself or to Spirit.

❧ You know there's a reason for being here. There is a purpose to your life, and events don't happen to you randomly.

❧ You're asking not to be fixed, or for the world to be changed. You're asking for the healing of anything that stands in your way of being a full expression of light.

❧ You're realizing that your thoughts create your experience here, and that by working with Spirit, you can change the thoughts that interfere with your peace and happiness.

❧ You acknowledge that you deserve to have inner peace. By asking for anything that stands in the way of peace to be healed, you claim that you deserve it, and that Spirit wants you to be joyful. You do this for the good of yourself and the world.

Now that you've started the conversation, how do you deepen the relationship? The Law of Attraction says that you focus on what you want, and you will draw it to you. This has sometimes been misinterpreted as a cosmic vending machine. You put in your request, and what you asked for pops right out. In truth, the fulfillment of desire takes place within a larger conversation that's collaborative and develops over time.

It's easy to turn to guidance when you're in a crisis, or to be wowed by meeting your guides for the first time. But think of the importance of relationship in human terms. We can benefit from going on a date, but we grow on a deep level when we wake up next to the same person day after day. We can learn from a two-hour workshop, but our lives change dramatically when we commit to a one-year course.

This is about intentionally developing a mutually beneficial relationship. It will take some time—though little effort—on your part, and it will be one of the most rewarding relationships of your life.

So what qualifications do you need? If you're breathing, you're in. If you haven't been to church in twenty years—or ever—you're in. If you've served time, you're in. If you consider yourself the most ordinary, unremarkable person (and I assure you that you're not), you're in.

In other words, you don't have to go to seminary, be born again, or profess faith in any way to any thing to earn a relationship with your guides. You just have to listen. I'll show you how.

Over the centuries, mystics were considered a rare group of people who could talk to God directly. That made us think that they had special powers—probably unattainable powers. But the truth is, we all have that same ability to talk to Spirit. We just don't know how to use it. And if you think you don't want to be a mystic or you're afraid of mystical ability because it's too much responsibility, ask for your fears about it to be healed.

Being a mystic in my book means that you're aware of energy or a presence beyond our five senses, and you make an effort to communicate in some way. When you do that, you'll start having mystical experiences. Not crazy, unpredictable séance and Ouija board experiences, but everyday part-of-life experiences.

As my mentor and friend Dorothy used to say, "Some people are so spiritual that they're no earthly good." In other words, the goal of the mystic is not to denounce our human-ness, but to remember that there's more available to us than what we can see in physical form.

In meeting and building a relationship with your guides, you may start to feel a comforting presence. You may have significant dreams. You may receive strong impressions about what you should or shouldn't do. You may feel a sense of

"

*Once you claim
your inner mystic,
life will never
be the same.*

"

protection. You may stand at the dishwasher and hear something as mundane as "Sears."

Make time for this relationship, just as you would for your children or friends. Wear your title of "mystic" proudly. Take walks in the woods to listen. Honor messages as they come. And as your ego pops up to discredit them, ask for your fear-based thoughts to be healed. Get a t-shirt that says, "I'm a mystic with mushroom soup casseroles."

Do whatever it takes to acknowledge and elevate this role in your life. Because, believe me, once you claim your inner mystic, life will never be the same.

Opening Up to
Spiritual Guidance

Many years ago, I attended a workshop that included several creative exercises designed to help us dream of possibilities in our lives. I didn't know it at the time, but those exercises laid a foundation for my understanding of how we communicate with one another as humans—and non-humans—and the knowledge we can draw on when we open our minds.

For one exercise, the leader had us sit around a table with three complete strangers. Since there were close to two hundred people in the room, this was not a problem. Then she gave us our instructions.

"I want one of you to turn away from the table so your back is to the group," she said. "The other three of you at the table . . . you talk about the person who is facing away from you. Talk about that person for three minutes."

We all looked at each other. What did she mean, *talk* about that person? What was there to talk about? We'd just met each other. We knew absolutely nothing.

Other people in the room had the same question, and several hands shot up in the air.

"Just try it," she said. "See what comes out of your mouths. When you finish talking about one person, the next person can turn away from the table. Keep going until you've talked about each person. Ready?"

No, we weren't.

"Go."

We all looked at each other thinking *What do we do now?* Then a young woman at our table said, "Okay, I'll turn around."

She was attractive and professionally dressed. No distinguishing features or habits. But we simply started talking about her. And for some reason, one of the people at our table said, "She's a drum majorette."

Yeah, that was good. A drum majorette. "She leads parades," we said. "In fact, she's led a parade down 5th Avenue in Manhattan." The story kept growing as we grabbed the thread and pulled.

After three minutes, the young woman turned around. Her face was pale. "How did you know?" she said. "I *have* led parades. I *am* a majorette."

Whoa. *That* was a fluke. We chalked it up to a lucky guess.

It was my turn.

I rotated my chair away from the table and listened as the strangers described me.

"She's an artist or a writer," one of them said.

"Yeah," said another. "She likes adventure, especially climbing pyramids and exploring the jungle."

Now, I'm guessing I looked about as far from an adventurer as you can imagine, given that I was probably wearing some buttoned-up midwestern top and a decent pair of slacks, and my hair was carefully shellacked with hairspray.

Nothing about my appearance gave away the fact that I'd just returned from a trip to Mexico, where I'd been researching Mayan pyramids in the jungles of the Yucatán Peninsula.

Now we all had goose bumps.

It still seemed like sheer accident, but as we continued the exercise with the two men at our table, we were equally accurate. Yes, one *had* been a bullfighter (in the interest of full disclosure, the gentleman is Hispanic, but the bullfighting story still seemed like a leap) and, yes, the other rode dirt bikes in the mountains. Somehow we just knew.

Clearly, something beyond us was going on here. This was no party trick. We had tapped into something beyond our five senses, even though not one of us had any special psychic abilities.

I tell you this as an example of how natural it is to draw information from beyond our five senses when fear is not in the way. There was no pressure to be right—at least not at first. We simply opened up to information and received it. And we did it collectively, each building on one another's guidance.

If we can receive such information about complete strangers, just think what's possible when we open up to guidance about ourselves.

The term "spiritual guidance" covers a broad range of definitions and beliefs. Some people call it intuition. Artists often refer to it as their muse. Others think of spiritual guidance as angels, God, or an energy flow or vibration that's beyond religion and doesn't depend on belief in a specific deity.

Our brains aren't wired to recognize things we don't have names for. That's why the simple act of saying "I receive spiritual guidance" can help open you up to receiving it in the way that's right for you.

This is my understanding: We each have one or more guides who have been with us since before we were born. They're our

"

There is no one who does not have helpers who are eager to work with and support them more directly and consciously.

"

team, and they're with us constantly. The team may change as we learn and grow, but they are here with us always to give us direction and support, accessing a much bigger picture than we can possibly see through our limited human eyes.

One of the things that happens when you co-create with your guides is that you step into what has become known as authentic power—the unique alchemy of spiritual light and strength that you brought into this world. Your guides don't just help you decide whether to quit your job or how to handle a tough situation with your kids. They help you fulfill the promise of who you are.

Their focus, in other words, is not on helping you make a million dollars. Their focus is on helping you shed all the fears that keep you from being the powerful and compassionate and funny and extraordinary cosmic recipe that bears your name. And as you do that, making a million dollars may (or may not) be a byproduct.

Along the way, they'll help you claim your innate beauty, see everything as a gift, give yourself and everybody else a break, and keep growing until the day you leave your body behind. They will help you go beyond the life you hoped you'd have to the life you never even imagined. And they will do it not according to your schedule, but according to a schedule that actually makes sense: when you're ready, and not a nanosecond before.

This is soul-to-soul guidance, best explained by one who sees a bigger picture than I do. That's why I posed the question to my writing guide.

"Ella, what is spiritual guidance?"

Spiritual guidance is the ability to listen to and be directed by your spirit guides consciously. You are always receiving guidance, a flow of energy and thought that can give you concrete and practical steps to take in your life. This is what people don't understand. They may think of spiritual guidance as inspiration or a gut feeling, which it certainly can be. But we are not so far removed from your physical human experience that we don't understand the everyday decisions you deal with in physical form.

As you know from your own experience, we can tell you whether to turn right or left, where to go next, what to do on your to-do list, who to talk to, and what to say. We are intimately involved with those serendipitous events that you attribute to the universe, and the God moments in which there's a flash of knowledge or peace that passeth understanding. What we want to get across is that truly we are here with you always, and while you may not always feel our presence directly, that doesn't mean we aren't here.

If the communication is blocked, it's never because we have blocked it. It is always fear that stands in the way, and it is healing the fear that opens the lines of communication. As your friend once said, "Now we can really get things done!"

We are eager to work with you as direct partners, and we honor you. You are not lesser than us. You are not lower beings. You are, in fact, courageous souls who are navigating the Earth plane and all the human emotions of fear that can make your experience seem so fretful and challenging and sad. We honor all these experiences and the growth they can bring. And at the same time, we are here to help you have more joy and abundance in your life, more ease, because your life experience does not require struggle or pain.

The more you work with us, the easier your life may become. Not because you won't still have challenges, but because together we can help you see them in new ways and heal from them faster. We can instill in you a sense of purpose that makes it exciting to wake up in the morning. We can pave the way for your days to be easier and more abundant and filled with joy by helping you make decisions that can lift you up and traverse obstacles. We can help you experience your human life as an adventure . . . a chance to explore other worlds, other cultures, without judgment or expectations that can make you miserable or feel cheated.

This is what we're here for with every one of you.

There is no one who does not have helpers who are eager to work with and support them more directly and consciously.

Set aside time every day to talk to us in some form, and we will be there for the conversation with delight. This is real, not an imagining. And there is no one who does not deserve our help.

At this point I asked Ella, "What about people who don't believe they deserve it?"

If you believe that you do not deserve our help, you are confusing your identity with your fear. You are a child of God who took on a body and a life situation so you could grow and experience this physical world for one purpose only: to extend more love into this world, remembering who you are as a child of God and strengthening that in yourself. This is a holy and sacred purpose.

Your purpose and identity are not your job or where you live or what you own. Your purpose and identity are to extend divine love. You do these things in a way that's different from everyone around you because you have unique skills and abilities. But in the end, your purpose is love. Hey, that's our purpose too! Let's work together, and we can extend it faster and more effectively. We respect and admire you, and we are honored to call you our friend.

You are taught that this human experience is supposed to be hard, and you make it that way because of all the expectations you bring to it. People are supposed to live long lives. They're supposed to have a certain amount of money in the bank. They are not supposed to die before their parents. They're not supposed to have serious health conditions. They're successful if they can retire and have a vacation at the end of their lives. Some skin colors are better than others. Driving a certain car makes you a superior person.

Do you see the insanity in these statements? This is why you need us. Because you're living in a world ruled by fear, in which your existence is defined by parameters that fear created. If you try to live within that world without guidance, you will feel the insanity eating you away.

With guidance, you will remember who you are. You will be reminded that it's perfectly okay to not meet the world's expectations because they're not what you're designed for. You will experience a freedom, a burden lifted from your shoulders so that you're no longer living someone else's life, but you're living the one that is yours to live.

This is our job, it is what we stand beside you to do: to help you live your life in a way that is a full and unique expression of your soul as you bring love into this world. To help when you get stuck or afraid. To pave the way to make life easier to navigate. To remind you that all is well even when you can't see the whole picture. To bring the people into your life who will help you grow. To open you up to imagining and remembering all of who you are.

It is our honor to do so. All you have to do is ask.

"

All you have

to do is ask.

"

How I Met My Guides

When I was in fifth grade, I was invited to a slumber party. I desperately wanted just one thing: a pair of Jolly Green Giant slippers to arrive in time for the event. They looked like something an elf would wear: green felt slippers with zigzag edges and turned-up toes. I had ordered them through the mail with a canned corn proof-of-purchase label and a few cents for shipping.

In my ten-year-old mind, it was *very* important to have those slippers for the party. They were unique and trendy (I thought) in a fifth-grader sort of way. I'd be the only one at the sleepover with such cool elf wear.

The slippers had not arrived by the day of the event. My mom was taking me to the slumber party at noon, so I paced the floor in my room, pleading for those slippers to come before we left. I was so *clear* about wanting them, so genuine in my request.

At 11:55 a.m., with just five minutes to spare, the mailman came. And there, lo and behold, was a small box with a picture of the Jolly Green Giant on it.

I don't remember a thing about wearing those slippers at the party (or how the other girls must have rolled their eyes), but the message was not lost on me: prayers are answered. I had a sense that I'd asked, and someone had responded. I wasn't certain God had been personally involved in arranging the shipping and handling, though, since I was pretty sure He had other things to do. But something—someone who felt familiar to me—was working on my behalf.

Even as I write this now, many (many!) years later, my ego wants to rise up, waving the flag of coincidence and discounting the slippers' delivery as a well-timed accident.

But the seed of awareness and faith that was planted all those years ago took root and has grown ever since. Sometimes it has blossomed, at times it has been dormant. But ultimately that seed has been strong enough to weather drought, hail, and fierce winds because, from that moment on, I knew somewhere deep inside that I was not alone.

A FEW YEARS LATER, when I was sixteen, another seemingly small miracle gave me a similar feeling of support, rescuing me from an adolescent depression.

In those few short years since the Jolly Green Giant slippers, I'd followed the same trajectory of so many adolescents. I'd gone from celebrating my right to be different to feeling disconsolate because I *was* different.

I sat on my twin bed at home, feeling terribly lonely. My brothers and sisters were off at college, the girls from my fifth-grade class had long ago made other friends, and my best friend had joined the ranks of flag twirlers and softball players—groups that were not a good match for my social and physical awkwardness. Dating was out of the question—I was far too good in English class for that. Plus, I froze every time a boy came within ten feet of me.

I felt I didn't belong anywhere, and I wasn't willing to talk about my loneliness to anyone. I didn't tell my parents. I didn't tell anybody much of anything. I just listened to myself a lot, and the messages generally were not good.

That particular night, I sat in my blue quilted bathrobe on the flowered bedspread my mom had made. I was in one of the safest places on Earth—in Des Moines, Iowa, in a neighborhood of tidy brick homes called Beaverdale, in a bedroom decorated with the oranges and yellows and lime greens of the early 1970s, with two parents who were good to one another sleeping a floor below me.

The secure environment around me seemed inconsequential. I was so miserable, I cried before I laid out a solitaire game as a way to settle down for the night. The fact that I was playing solitaire—a game for one—was not lost on me. I said what I would not have called a prayer, because I didn't really pray. But it sure sounded like a prayer, since it was addressed right to the heart of God.

Basically, I poured out my misery. How much I felt like an outsider and a social misfit. How much I wanted friendship and a sense of connection. And mostly, how much I wanted to like myself. Not just to respect my academic abilities, but to really like being me—whoever that was.

Half feeling disconsolate and half feeling relieved to have shared my burden, I began playing that first game of solitaire on the flowered bedspread. I laid one column of cards on another and turned over new plays, and before long all the cards lined up on the aces. I'd won. Great.

I laid out another game. A different kind of solitaire, a little more challenging. A couple of minutes later, *ta-da*. Everything fell into place, and I won again.

The third game was yet another form of solitaire (we played a lot of cards in my family). I won again. Highly unusual.

34

"

*Divine love rearranged **me**, restacking the blocks so they wouldn't tumble.*

"

The fourth time, I started to realize something besides me was in charge of the cards. I felt something soften inside. I'd never had a string of wins like this before.

The fifth time, when all the cards lined up at the end once again, I got it.

"Thank you," I said to whoever was listening. I looked up and around me, and I'm guessing that I turned slightly to my right, toward the lime green dresser my mom had painted to go with the flowered bedspread. Slightly to the right seems to be the telephone line to my primary guide, even though I didn't know it at the time.

I set aside the cards, folded up my eyeglasses, and said a silent "thank you." I felt a sense of reassurance, as if someone had put their arm around my shoulder and dabbed at my cheeks with a handkerchief. I pulled up the flowered bedspread around my shoulders and fell asleep.

Within a few weeks, friends started showing up, and I've been blessed with an abundance of deep friendships ever since. I thought at the time that it was just God's magic, sending people to me in response to my prayer. Now, all these years later, I realize that God did perform a miracle that night, but it wasn't in rearranging the social schedules of the people around me.

Divine love rearranged *me*, restacking the blocks so they wouldn't tumble.

My guides reassured me of my own sense of safety and security in the world, the place where everything starts.

CLEARLY, NEITHER THE Jolly Green Giant slippers nor the solitaire games would be termed a miracle in most people's minds. There was no sweeping drama, nothing that would make someone gasp and stand in awe at what they'd just witnessed. Just a young girl in her bedroom asking for help and receiving it in the most subtle and gentle of ways.

But that *was* the miracle.

Our ability to co-create with Spirit mirrors our ability to do the same thing with each other in this human experience. In human form, we express our affection and support and comfort for one another in the simplest and most mundane ways: a touch, a note to say "I'm thinking of you," a pot of soup, or a plate of brownies. Our relationship with Spirit is much the same. That's one of the most important things I've learned: if we expect help from Spirit to arrive with the sound of trumpets and blinding light, we'll overlook all the nuanced help that's delivered in small ways every day.

In fact, one of the wisest things I've ever heard came from a friend named Steve. Steve was a recovering alcoholic, and he had attended retreats at a monastery in eastern Iowa—an

"

If we expect help from Spirit to arrive with the sound of trumpets, we'll overlook all the nuanced help that's delivered in small ways every day.

"

exquisitely simple limestone building on a hill, bordered by trees on one side and farm fields on the other. The chapel was lined with stone, and the sound of the early morning chants rose up to the roof and filled every crevice with grace.

When a friend and I decided to go there for a personal retreat one weekend, I asked Steve what I should wear.

He looked at me, puzzled. Not realizing that he was about to rock my world, he said, "It doesn't matter. If you worry about what you're wearing, you'll miss the miracle."

HERE'S THE THING. We expect miracles to be about the form: what we're wearing, the heroic act, the Bible saved in a tornado. All of those things are about our physical existence. But the real miracle is the change that happens in our minds. A natural occurrence of love. A change in perception.

This happened for me the day I met my spirit guides about twenty years ago. I visited a woman in Des Moines who was a clinical psychologist and who also performed past-life regressions. In one session, I returned to the place between worlds. The place we "inhabit" before we are born into this life.

There, standing in front of me like a team of cosmic cheerleaders, were my guides. They wore white jogging pants and sweatshirts with a red letter on their chests that I couldn't identify. They were animated, excited, happy to show me how supportive they were and to communicate so directly. They wanted me to know why I was on Earth, what I had come here to do, and how I could fulfill the contract I'd helped write before birth.

I asked why I had been born in the Midwest, and they showed me the Earth as though I was looking at it from the moon. It was covered with strands of energy, like a ball of yarn. Those were strands of divine love, they said. But the strands didn't just encircle the Earth, they also ran *through* the Earth like roots that connected one side of the planet and one pole to the other, delivering the energy of spiritual nourishment.

Then one guide got down on one knee and extended one arm in the air behind him and the other out straight in front of him. I saw a ball of energy roll down the uplifted arm and shoot out toward the Earth along his outstretched arm, moving fast, like he was catapulting it toward the Earth.

"That's the energy of love," they said. "You're here to bring love into this world as fast as possible."

It was time for me to help do that, they said. Do it through writing, through sharing ideas, through talking about planting seeds and spiritual growth. Do it by expressing love in your own life. More and more people are needed to talk about

"

The real miracle is the change that happens in our minds. A natural occurrence of love. A change in perception.

"

these ideas, they reminded me. This is how the world will move forward, how we'll bridge the gap between spirituality and science, how we'll acknowledge each person's potential to heal and be healed.

Despite the fact that I knew they were right, a familiar terror had been building within me as I watched, anticipating how vulnerable I would feel, how ridiculous I might look. I reverted back to my sixteen-year-old self, sitting on my bed, afraid of being rejected.

Unexpectedly, I burst into tears.

"Don't make me go out there," I said.

But I knew it was time. A shift occurred in my thinking when I saw those guides and the help they provide. I knew they'd been there my whole life, nudging and supporting and carrying me. And now they were asking me to step up and do what I came here to do.

And I said yes.

That was the miracle. The miracle wasn't that I saw them or that they spoke to me directly. The miracle was that, in my awareness of them, my perception changed. I took a step forward. I moved from fear to love.

That journey is the essence of the mystical, co-creative relationship. We take it not by stopping a moving train or throwing ourselves in front of a speeding bullet. We do it by listening. Listening when we are joyful. Listening when we're sad. Taking note of the "coincidences" and the "hidden" messages in our everyday lives.

And, ultimately, by saying yes.

How Do We Communicate?

My friend John is a professor of business, a former CEO, and a member of one of the country's largest churches, although he considers himself a spiritual person rather than a religious one.

In 2006, he was sitting in a hotel room in Phoenix, getting ready for a second-year doctoral residence, and he needed to present his dissertation topic the next day. There was just one small problem.

"I didn't have any idea what my project would be about," he says.

While he sat in that hotel room, he heard a voice, which he recognized as his angel. "She said, 'Your topic is ethical intelligence.'" John googled the topic and found six hundred hits online, but none of them fit the description of what his angel had told him. So he put together a proposal based on the angel's guidance and presented it to his colleagues the next day.

"Everybody was highly intrigued," John says. "But my professor said it would be a tough topic to handle and suggested I do something a little less grandiose."

He tried. Over the next twelve months he explored other topics. "But every time, my angel would come back and say again, 'Your topic is ethical intelligence.'"

Then something happened that clinched the deal. John was reading scripture one morning, and a dragonfly came and hovered over his Bible. Immediately after, he heard a voice that changed the name in the verse to *his* name: "The hands of John have laid the foundation of this truth. His hands shall also finish it . . ."

"That's when I *knew* I had to do the ethical intelligence project," he says. He wrote a note in his Bible that said "Time to publish." Now, not only has he completed his dissertation, but he's turning it into a book for business leaders, and it promises to be a landmark work.

"I've been guided the whole time to the right resources," he says. "The more I worked on the project, the more I allowed myself to open to it. The more messages I get, the stronger they are."

Clearly, this isn't a surprise to John, given that he begins each day by reading, praying, and meditating. "I welcome in spirits that want to come in and help me," he says. "And often they do."

If he had any doubt, he could just ask his granddaughter, who walked into his office when she was three years old and said, "Papa, I see all these angels."

JOHN IS THE PERFECT EXAMPLE of what can happen when you build a relationship with your own personal guidance through consistent study, daily invitations, attentive listening, and acting on the answers you receive.

His story also showcases an array of delivery systems that the guides use for their communication, including messages in nature, the voices of angels and guides, and persistent nudges toward essential information.

Working with spiritual guidance, like any relationship, looks different for different people. We all bring our unique personality traits and intentions to our interactions, and so do they.

I was reminded of this when I did a presentation about co-creating with Spirit, and during the question and answer time at the end, one woman asked this question: "Whenever

"

*Working with
spiritual guidance,
like any relationship,
looks different for
different people.*

"

I talk with my guides, they ask me to order a pizza. What should I do?"

Hmmm. I can honestly say that my guides have never requested food. But I told her, "Order a large supreme." Honestly. How better to build a close relationship?

Some people can see their guides, while others hear them or receive communication through automatic writing. The communication can be as simple as a symbol in nature, repeated patterns of numbers, flickering lights, a particular odor or fragrance, or an affirmative tingle when you hear something that just feels right. There's no "right" way to communicate.

It begins, of course, by simply saying hello. From there you can go many different ways, and it's helpful to experiment to see which works best for you.

Building a relationship with your guides is the same as sitting down with your grandmother or an old teacher from childhood and having a conversation. Be discerning. If something doesn't feel right or true, know that that's part of the collaboration process. Ask your guides why you're feeling that way.

Know that your ego will try to sideswipe you over and over again, and that it may take a while to build trust in your own ability to hear or receive communication. This is because, from the time we were little and first mentioned an imaginary friend, we've been taught not to trust it. Your ego will reinforce that distrust over and over again.

Also, remember that you'll experience exactly what's right for you. A friend, for instance, often experiences her guidance through music, art, and nature. When she started thinking she "should" actually converse with her guides, she woke up one morning and heard a radio-like sound of a lot of people talking at once. She sat up, looked around for the source of the noise, and received this message: "Really? Is this what you want? Relax. Our way of communicating with you is fine." The noise disappeared, and she hasn't questioned their communication style since.

With that in mind, here are a few ways to get started.

Write down your experiences.

Writing is an excellent way to talk with your guides, especially at the beginning, because it allows you to listen and document your experience simultaneously. Sit at the computer or in a quiet place with pen and paper, and simply ask a question. Then record whatever sensations, insights, pictures, words, colors, or sounds come along.

"

Remember that you'll experience exactly what's right for you.

"

When you see those words on paper afterward, there's no denying that *something* occurred. It may be nonsensical at first, but the messages will become clearer as you develop the equivalent of more bandwidth. It's important to preserve this kind of record to quiet your ego, which will tell you that you're making it all up.

Consider keeping all your spirit guide communication in a special journal or set of computer files as a way of honoring the messages. This will also make them easier to revisit from time to time.

Visualize meeting with your guides.

Visualizations can be extremely effective because they open up the third eye and allow you to see pictures or actions as though you're watching a video.

To do this, imagine that you're meeting your guide at a predetermined spot. Make it a place where you feel comfortable. See yourself welcoming your guide into your home or sitting together on a park bench, or in whatever setting you choose. Ask to be able to see and understand the conversation. Then pose questions and become aware of what you hear. It's an excellent idea to write down what you experience afterward.

Again, know that the quality may be fuzzy at first, and you may feel like the video is buffering. Over time, this will change, allowing you to view your conversations with more clarity and depth.

Meet your guides in your dreams.

Before you go to bed at night, simply ask to meet your guides in your dreams, and to remember that meeting when you wake up in the morning.

Your dream may look very different than you expect, so let go of expectations and find the meaning in what's presented to you rather than trying to dictate the form or type of meeting you'll have. For example, you may request a meeting and then have a dream in which two children are climbing up and down shelves in a crowded warehouse. When you awaken and think about the dream, write down as much as you can remember. Then ask questions about it. *Why were we in a warehouse? What does the warehouse represent? Why were we children? What was in the boxes? Why were we climbing?* Think about any details—even if they seem insignificant—and ask what they mean.

Also, if you have an issue or problem you're trying to work out, ask your guides for their input before you go to sleep, then check in for the answer when you wake up. My husband

Bob does this frequently, giving new meaning to the phrase "let me sleep on it."

Clear your mind with meditation.

Typically in meditation, the goal is to clear your mind of thought until you achieve a feeling of nothingness—an empty mind. By allowing your mind to drift and relax, you make yourself available for instruction and conversation.

I tend not to use this technique very often simply because I get so relaxed that I can't remember much of my interaction with the guides. Since I'm typically focused on information and being able to share it, this is not concrete enough for me, but it may be perfect for you. And it's an excellent way to ask for an energetic shift and then allow it to happen while you're deeply relaxed.

Open your mind with physical activity.

A channeler friend of mine uses regular playing cards when he's doing a reading. He doesn't look for information in the cards. Instead, he shuffles and lays them out in patterns while he's speaking, simply because the physical act of touching the cards helps free his mind so he can listen for information. This is the same reason many school counselors keep a collection of tactile toys in their offices. When kids come in, sit down, and turn the toys over and over in their hands, they relax, open up, and have a deeper conversation.

When you do something physical that doesn't require decision-making or focus, you free your mind to communicate with Spirit. Gardening, cleaning, walking, and other free-form activities provide natural openings for conversation. Pose a question in your mind, then keep a piece of paper or your phone voice recorder handy so you can jot down or record important insights.

Enjoy the natural world.

Being outdoors immediately reminds us, consciously or unconsciously, that we're part of a vast system of energy that carries intelligence, wisdom, and complexity beyond our understanding. Your spiritual guidance can use any element of nature—from a leaf to a bird to the setting sun or a sky filled with stars—for direct communication.

A young woman who I'll call Maria discovered this in one of our workshops a few years ago. Her mother had died in a car accident when Maria was a child. The lingering fear and grief over that loss now was interfering with her ability to be the mother she wanted to be. When she took a walk during our

"

Like any relationship, your relationship with Spirit is based on trust.

"

workshop on a cold January day, she saw a tree that was completely bare except for one leaf. When she rejoined the group, she seemed more at peace than she had been earlier in the day.

"That leaf has been hanging on too long," she said, "and so have I." That single moment of awareness and release started her on a new path, helping her relinquish a long-standing fear. It was a moment of profound guidance, prompted by the symbolism of nature.

LIKE ANY RELATIONSHIP, your relationship with Spirit is based on trust. You have to trust that you have guidance, trust the information you receive, and trust that it will show up for you. Most importantly, you have to trust yourself to show up, too.

Once you know the preferred method of communication with your guides, ask them why that's best. Why do you hear an internal voice rather than seeing shapes? Why do you feel nudges rather than remembering your dreams? There's a reason your window to their world was designed a certain way, and it will alleviate the ego's communication envy if you learn why and how it's perfect for you.

That's my take on it. But Ella said it better. Here are her thoughts.

There is no one way or right way to communicate with your guides. Just as you have many forms of communication in your physical world, so there are many apertures and openings to the nonphysical available to you. It is extremely important to release any expectations about how the communication should function, as this will simply impede the process.

Please know that you have avenues of communication with your guidance that were set up before you were born, and they are as unique to you as your fingerprints. If you start coveting another person's form of communication, you abdicate your own. It would be like coveting another person's DNA. Instead, become curious about your own mode of communication. Study it. Appreciate it. Celebrate it with your guides. Rather than judging it, learn why it is perfect for your soul growth.

First, ask your guides what the best way would be to communicate with them. You can do this simply by sitting quietly, without any distractions, after taking several deep breaths. State your intention in your mind to connect with your guides and to get to know them. Then sit quietly and pay attention. You may feel a brush of your shoulder. You may have a sense of presence. You may see something in your mind's eye. You may hear an internal voice. You may feel energy moving through you in a subtle but evident way.

Pay attention to anything, no matter how nuanced, and suspend the ego's need to discount it, as that's exactly what it will do. Take note of anything you feel or experience and write it down so that you are giving it credence and can remember it, as the ego will try to erase it from your mind entirely.

Do this for several days in a row, at the same time each day. Your intention to set up a regular meeting time with your spiritual guidance will give you a sense of expectation and accountability, and it will show your guides that you have the beginnings of a commitment to building this relationship. Each day, note whatever you experience, no matter how slight. Do you notice any changes from day to day? Do you have a sense of a message being delivered to you? It's perfectly okay if the answers are no. Just keep showing up and demonstrating your willingness and availability.

At some point, you will have a breakthrough. It is impossible to predict when this will happen. However, if you use the invitation [in Chapter 8] you will experience a response more readily. Congratulations. You have just opened up to the most vast and reliable and helpful and loving resource you will ever have.

When you do, start asking questions just as you would a friend who you're getting to know.

◊ Tell me about yourself.

◊ I want to know more about you.

◊ What do you care about the most?

◊ Why have we come together?

◊ How can you help me?

◊ How can I help you?

◊ What is the best way to communicate?

◊ When would we like to get together?

Think of the first transcontinental telephone line. It opened a window for communication that never seemed possible before. Now that connection has advanced to the airwaves, without need for physical cables or lines. This is a model of what's possible between our world and yours. You are simply stringing energetic cable from our world to yours, connecting in a way you never thought possible before, even though everything that was needed has been there all along.

You might also think of it as living in a house within a few feet of another home. When your windows are closed and the drapes drawn, you are unaware of that other house. But when you draw back the drapes and open the window, you can talk easily from one house to another.

This is all we're asking you to do. It is no more complex or magical than this. We are all together whether you see or experience us or not. We are right next door whether you're aware or not. And wouldn't life be easier if you were aware?

Imagine that the neighbor you have been unaware of is just the person you need to introduce you to a new community and get you a new job and introduce you to the love or your life and give you excellent advice when you are dispirited or discouraged or confused.

Imagine that this neighbor, because she has been living in this neighborhood for so long, understands the lay of the land completely. She knows what happened forty years ago and has a good idea what will happen forty years from now and can give you guidance that will help point you in the right direction. She can see the big picture that you can't. Her house sits atop a hill, so she can see when storms are coming and can help you prepare for them or shift so that they miss you entirely.

Imagine that this is a great aunt who has loved you since before you were born but has been unknown to you. She is so happy to finally have a real relationship with you, and while she understands your skepticism and resistance at first, she welcomes you with open arms and wants you to understand that she wants only the best for you. And nothing would make her happier than to devote all her time to helping you, because this would fulfill her mission and sense of purpose. She knows that by helping you, her work is done, because you can go out and be her hands and feet and voice and ears and eyes.

This is what's available to you simply by sitting for a few minutes each day, asking and listening. It is an exchange of riches, is it not? And it is the easiest thing in the world, for there is literally nothing for you to do but to sit, be quiet, ask questions in your mind, and listen for the answers.

Here is what will happen over time when you start this process and become regular about it.

◊ You will start to look forward to it.

◊ There will be the same sense of anticipation you would have if you were meeting a favorite friend for lunch.

◊ When you have questions, you will start turning to your spiritual guidance rather than looking for answers in the external world.

◊ You will understand yourself and other people in ways you never have before.

◊ You will understand your own fears and those of others like never before.

◊ You will feel less lonely. How can you feel abandoned when you know you're never alone?

◊ You will enjoy spending time with yourself more.

◊ You will focus more on what is going right in your life rather than what is going wrong.

◊ You will start seeing new meaning in life events for yourself and others.

◊ You will stop measuring success by dollars and material things and instead define it in terms of soul growth.

◊ You will see your life purpose unveiled to you day by day.

◊ You will bypass dead ends in relationships, jobs, and other areas of life, taking decisive action toward the life of your dreams.

◊ You will receive insights that will turn past trauma into an opportunity for growth.

◊ You will feel the arms of Spirit around you whenever you're disheartened, reminding you that you are pure light.

All of these things and more are available to you simply by saying yes to our partnership. Honestly, that's all it takes. You can still carry skepticism if you like, although that does nothing but make your ego happy and get in the way of quicker communication. Ask for your fear-based thoughts to be healed as they come up, and your relationship will build much more quickly.

Just like any relationship, this one will grow and mature and evolve over time. It will become one of the grandest adventures

"

Just like any relationship, this one will grow and mature and evolve over time.

"

of your life as you explore your inner world so you may bring that curiosity and wonder and exuberance to your life in the outer world.

We will surprise and delight you. We will confound you. We will challenge you. We will test your trust. We will provoke your ego. But always we will do it with your growth in mind. We will comfort and guide and uplift you. And remember, we are here with you always. The window is always open on our side, even if it seems closed on yours.

Guidance or Ego, Love or Fear?

As you start working with your guides, don't underestimate your ego's tenacity in discouraging and dissuading
you. Building this relationship truly is one of the easiest, most
helpful endeavors of your life, it costs you no money whatso-
ever, and the time is always rewarding. So the question is, why
isn't everybody doing it? And the answer is: the ego stands in
the way.

The ego is right there at the door saying, *Don't trust yourself
or any inner voice except mine.* It does this because it knows a relationship with Spirit will destroy its identity.

The fear-based ego keeps us distracted and focused on the
physical world, convincing us that we're small and insignificant. It wants us to believe that we're separate from God. So
what is it going to fear more than anything else? Anything that

"

The fear-based ego keeps us distracted and focused on the physical world.

"

reminds us we're *not* separate from God—that, in fact, we are expressions and extensions of divine love. The biggest threat of all to your ego is a relationship with your spirit guides that means you're relying on their loving direction rather than all the ego's demands.

The ego will do its craziest dance around you. *Maybe it's time for a nap . . . for the next few days. Or, hey, how about if you get sick— really, really sick, and then you'll be so focused on how your head hurts or your stomach aches or the endless stream of snot coming out of your nose that you certainly won't be listening to Spirit.*

Your ego will come up with all sorts of different ways to keep you from building a relationship with your guides, so be intentional and consistent, and be aware as these distractions come up, understanding what they are and where they come from.

With that said, one of the first things the ego will do is try to convince you not to trust. *Those messages you keep getting? They're just your imagination. Ignore those nudges of intuition. Don't pay attention to those recurring dreams about quitting your job or moving to a new house. Don't think that hearing the same obscure song three times in two days means anything.*

Your ego will also try to insert itself into the whole process of communicating with your guides. Because of this, it's important to start every interaction with a desire to be a neutral party so that your fears don't cloud what you experience. You might begin by saying, "Please heal my fear-based thoughts so I can receive your communication without interference." Also begin with a clearly stated intention to communicate only with the highest vibration of guidance possible. Be clear about the fact that you're not inviting or allowing any energy that's not for the highest good. By your presence and intention, you communicate only with those who will meet you in light.

This is an important step in dissuading any energies that might work against you, and it also will keep you from being overwhelmed.

My stepdaughter, for instance, shut down her ability to communicate with spirits for many years because she was bombarded by them. They dogged her like an invisible paparazzi—demanding, jostling for her attention, and draining her energy. They weren't necessarily dark spirits, but they were a constant distraction, making inner quiet impossible.

As soon as she learned how to set limits and ask only for guidance that served her highest good, the crowds disappeared, and she was able to work with Spirit in peace.

How do you know if you're hearing spiritual guidance or the voice of your ego? How do you know if it's legitimate and coming from love, or if it's the ego wearing sheep's clothing, trying to masquerade as your guide but keeping you small and fearful?

Here are a few important clues.

The ego is loud. Your guidance is quiet.

In working with my guides over the years, I've found that their collective voice is a little like an announcer on public radio: quiet, calm, unhurried. The ego, on the other hand, reminds me of a carnival barker: quick with a response, in your face, never lacking for something to say.

The ego can't sit or stay still for very long. As soon as you ask a question, it's typically going to jump out of its chair, run up to you, stick its nose in your face and tell you exactly what it thinks, often in the loudest and most insistent voice possible.

Messages from Spirit, on the other hand, often float in like a breeze. They're soft, gentle, and still, and they feel light, like a feather that's just passing through your awareness.

This is why it's important to sit quietly and settle into a deeper place in your mind, giving yourself time to adjust the dial and go deeper rather than accepting the first and most insistent voice you hear.

"

Messages from

Spirit often

float in

like a breeze.

"

Remember, the fearful ego is like a trick candle that won't go out. When you try to extinguish it, it disappears for a moment and then comes back. The more energy you expend on it, the more you're focused on the fear. That's why your job is not to eradicate or vanquish the fear. Instead, ask Spirit to heal it for you so you can focus on the *real* light instead.

Your guidance is always a voice for love.

Your guidance will always speak from kindness and compassion. It will not direct you to act out of fear. This is not to say that it won't encourage you to do something that makes you nervous. You'll often feel this way because the guides are nudging you to grow. But they won't encourage you to dislike, disrespect, or hate someone, to carry a grudge or to lash out in any way. Their guidance will always be in alignment with divine love.

Here's a quick but effective visualization you can use to *feel* that energy as you make decisions in your daily life.

Take a few deep breaths and relax, then see a light or flame inside your abdomen, just above the navel. This light represents your soul, your essence. Think about something you want, and bring it into the glow of that light. Now ask if your desire is in accordance with Spirit. Listen quietly. If it's not, bless it, ask for your fear-based thoughts to be healed, and ask what Spirit's will is for you instead.

*The tone of your guidance will be different
from your own voice.*

When you pay close attention to messages from Spirit, you usually recognize that the tone is different from your own. Maybe it's a bit more formal. Maybe it sounds like a person from another time or another country. The vocabulary may include words you don't typically use—or even words that you have to look up because you've never heard them before. This is helpful because it affirms a Source different from your ego mind.

Guidance is direct and clear.

When you pay attention to messages, ask yourself: Is there a crystalline quality about them? Do they feel like they're coming from a higher vibration? Are they simple and straightforward, clear and incisive?

I find that my guides use an economy of words and communicate in the most direct but gentle ways. The energy behind their messages is so kind and loving that it wakes you up without making you angry.

Years ago, a channeler conducted a group session for a study group I was in, and the comments the spirit guide made to each individual in the group were often startling, but precisely on point. They ranged from "Why are you pretending to be something you're not?" to "You can't find a new relationship until you leave the old one."

These were things we wanted to say to one another in the study group but didn't know how without causing hard feelings. When Spirit said them, though, the words came through with love.

Guidance is judgment free.

When Spirit speaks, you listen instead of getting defensive because you know you're not being attacked.

Guides convey messages without judgment, blame, anger, or coercion.

They speak the truth and leave it at that, without attachment. Then it's up to us to accept it and learn from it . . . or not. If we don't, the guides will arrange for another opportunity.

With time, you'll recognize how unique and remarkable this quality is. As humans with egos, we have a much harder time being neutral. But that quality comes through loud and clear with the guides.

"

Guides convey messages without judgment, blame, anger, or coercion.

"

*Guidance introduces you to new thoughts
and fresh perspectives.*

When I got divorced many years ago, I was despondent about all the years I thought I'd wasted. I was twenty-nine, had no children, and didn't trust that I'd ever find romantic love again. That's when I went to see a channeler for the first time, and what I heard woke me up to a completely new perspective.

Those years in my first marriage weren't a waste, Spirit said. Instead, I had taken an accelerated path to growth, and my marriage compressed decades of learning into a few short years.

This was a new concept to me at the time, and it taught me that everything in our lives is purposeful. No experience is ever wasted. This didn't erase the pain from the divorce, but it showed me that I could understand my experience in a whole new light.

That's what spirit guides do.

When I sit down to write and I ask my guides a question, I never know what I'm going to learn. I try to meet them with no expectations or preconceptions, opening my mind to whatever shows up. Frequently, it takes me by surprise. And when I'm done and I read over what I typed (because I usually don't remember afterward), I'm often amazed at what came out.

Pay attention to the nuances of your communication with your guides, and listen between the lines. Over time, you'll start to view this world from their perspective rather than the ego's, helping you more fully understand the purpose of your life and the peace that comes from partnering with Spirit.

What Does It Mean
to Co-Create?

Before *The Only Little Prayer You Need* was released, I was drawn to a marketing program that I knew would help promote the book once it was launched. The program was not inexpensive, and I hesitated about signing up. Unsure what to do, I asked my guides, expecting a simple yes or no. I should have known better. Their answer, as often happens, went a completely different direction than I had anticipated.

It was just four short words: "Have mercy on us."

What? Have mercy on us? What did *that* mean? This was about *me*, not them, right? And what did having mercy on *them* have to do with signing up for a marketing program? And why in the world would light beings need my mercy anyway?

These were all good questions, and the guides were happy to enlighten me, providing another of the great and unexpected lessons I've learned along the way. I thought writing the book was all about *my* growth, sharing *my* message. But "Have mercy on us" turned creation into co-creation.

"We are helping you," my guides said, "to move this message into the earth plane on a bigger level than has been done before in your experience, and it is a monumental job even from our standpoint. The concept of fear-based thoughts is so critical to human development, and this is the best opportunity we have had to make the message plain and simple for more people on the planet than have been reached by it before. So we ask for your mercy and help, just as we give ours to you."

As anyone who has experienced an *aha* shift knows, it's difficult to describe the immediate impact of that moment. It feels like driving down a highway, adhering to a certain set of expectations about how you're traveling and where you're going, when suddenly, based on one seemingly simple piece of information, the car makes a ninety-degree turn and takes you in a different direction. Not only are you surprised by the change, but you wonder how you couldn't have seen this obviously better route before.

This was one of those moments for me, when I finally and fully realized I was working as part of that NASA team in which

I was the astronaut and the group in the control room was my team of spirit guides. I'd spent a lot of time complaining every time my spacesuit felt a little pinched, when my role was really to help the ground crew carry out our *collective* mission.

I can't overstate to you how big of a change this is, and how important it is in building your relationship with your guides. We're talking *partnership* here, not servitude or separation.

Again, it's easy to see the parallel in human terms. If you want to grow, challenge yourself to follow your dreams. But if you want exponential growth, see your dreams as part of a greater mission, and work with your team to make sure the mission's goals are satisfied.

HERE IS THE STORY OF CO-CREATION, straight from Ella's mouth.

❧ We work with you from before you're born to develop a blueprint for a life that will provide the greatest growth for your soul. You are assigned a team. That team is with you always whether you're aware of it or not. How directly the team can be involved in your life depends on how much you ask. It is certainly not a straight path, since free will is an important part (art) of your existence.

It is very difficult for a team of guides to stand by and watch you make mistakes that could have been avoided if you had simply asked and listened. When I say it is difficult, it is simply because we know this need not be. At the same time, we see how much your soul grows from these decisions, and we support you no matter what choices you make.

This is important for you to know. We don't turn away or judge you or give up on you. We will never abandon you or leave you unguided.

This is true for everyone. No matter who you are, no matter where you are on the planet, no matter what you do, where you live, or what your name is, you have guides who love and cherish you.

Now, how do we co-create? What is this relationship? Let's think of Jean, a woman who wears red flannel and drives a tractor. Jean has short dark hair and is in her fifties. She has raised children and now has grandchildren. She is not widely traveled—in fact, she has rarely ventured far from her hometown. But she is a woman of faith, and she would like to know more about how she can work with Spirit for her own good and the good of her family and community.

I use Jean as an example because she may not seem like a likely one to explore mysticism and the co-creative possibilities with Spirit. She is firmly grounded, has seen hardship and difficulty in her life, and wants to understand the meaning of this life experience. And so, even though she is not devout in a particular religion, she knows

82

there is spirit in the land she farms and the animals she raises. She is curious. And she wants to leave a better life for her children and grandchildren.

How can someone like Jean understand this co-creative relationship?

This way: Jean's desire to leave a legacy of love is a mirror of her guides' desires to bring more love into this world. In one form or another, that is what all of you are here for. It may be through becoming more compassionate or creating new ways of communicating or making life easier for one another. There are as many forms of it as there are people on Earth. The point is that Jean's desire is in direct alignment with her guides. She wants to create more love in the world, and so do they. So by building a relationship as a mystic—communicating more clearly with her guides—she is satisfying their desire as well as her own, even though she may not know that.

Human beings are literally the hands and feet and voices and ears of love, channeled from beyond the veil. There are no exceptions to this. Even the serial murderer or the ISIS warrior is here to create more love. Sometimes this is done by acting out in a way that seems most fearful. But these actions can prompt more love as people respond. This is why it's so important to react to events and the energy around you not by the way society expects you to, but by how your guidance tells you to.

"

Remember this:

Judgment will breed

more judgment.

Forgiveness will breed

more forgiveness.

"

Remember this: Judgment will breed more judgment. Forgiveness will breed more forgiveness.

If you can keep those two ideas front and center in your mind, they will be beacons for you to follow in bringing more love into the world. And when you ask, we will help you do that.

You make things so terribly hard on yourselves. It doesn't have to be that way. If you could know all the things we can do for you, you would give up the struggle and enjoy your lives.

Just think of what you're struggling with today. Whatever it is, we can help you with it. Your ego will discount that and try to prevent you from even asking. Do it anyway.

And know that you don't have to see or hear or feel us in any way for our communication to be effective. We cannot say it strongly enough: Let go of any expectations of what your relationship with your guides will look like, or how you will communicate. Know that if you ask the question silently or out loud, and if you take time to quiet yourself to receive the answer, the communication will occur in the way that is right for you.

This is the meaning of co-creation, is it not?

How Can Your
Guidance Help You?

Years ago, I woke up one morning with a fascinating thought floating through my mind, no doubt planted there by my guides.

What if, the thought went, *we remembered that being in these human bodies in our earthly lives is equivalent to a cosmic vacation?*

A provocative question. It definitely woke me up. And then the guides *really* started talking to me.

"How do you act when you're on vacation?" they asked.

Well, I thought, *I don't take things so seriously. I'm much more present, enjoying whatever shows up. I may have an itinerary and a plan, but it's fluid. If something better comes along, I jump on it without worrying whether it's the right decision. I enjoy it simply for what it is.*

"What else?" they asked.

I observe and soak up the people and cultures around me without judging them, but with an intention to learn and appreciate them. I'm grateful for the experiences and what I get to see and do. I'm relaxed and don't think about the past or future. I focus on enjoying where I am right now. I don't worry about whether my entire life will hinge on any one decision. Now I was on a roll.

I expect to be delighted. I appreciate each new view around the next corner. I know that people will take care of me if I get lost or need help. And I know I always have a lifeline back home.

I realize it's easier if I travel light. And if I make an effort to talk to people and get to know them along the way, I'll learn amazing things.

I'm not attached to one place or one experience or one decision or thing, because I know it's all temporary and I'll be going back home. I know that the hotel I stay in or the rental car I drive doesn't define me. I realize that if I spend my time finding fault with the hotel or the bus driver or the public bathrooms, or wondering how I look on the beach, I'm not going to have much of a vacation. But if I approach each day with anticipation of what will happen next, a path of wonder will be laid out before me.

I know I'll get back home and look back on the vacation with a sense of fondness for all the things we got to do and how much I learned about myself and others along the way.

"And that," the guides told me, "is an excellent description of life."

This was another *aha* moment.

"

*If I could live as
though I'm on a
wondrous adventure,
I could experience life
differently.*

"

If I could live as though I'm on a wondrous adventure—the vacation of a lifetime, so to speak—I could experience life differently.

I could bring a more carefree but mindful perspective to every day. I could fill my life with experiences rather than things (even though a few souvenirs never hurt). I could go through my days with curiosity rather than judgment. And, most of all, I'd be aware that my mindset alone would either make the "vacation" exciting and growthful or filled with disappointments.

I tell you this for a couple of reasons. First, because the vacation model of life is powerful, and I encourage you to adopt it. And also, because when you develop a relationship with your guides, you start to receive more of these spontaneous teaching moments and shifts in perspective. Instead of simply asking them to help you find a job or heal your headache, you've granted them permission to let you in on universal secrets. Those insights can give you the confidence to take your foot off the brake and pick up momentum on your life path.

When I woke up the morning that the vacation thought was floating through my mind, I hadn't asked for a new perspective. But because I had a relationship with the guides, they knew I'd asked for continued growth, as though I'd signed up for a continuing education program that would never end.

Again, it's just like a human-to-human relationship. If you communicate infrequently and don't know each other well, the conversation tends to stay more on the surface. But when you commit to really knowing each other, you can get to the good stuff more quickly. You can hear them when they say, "You know, it's probably time to look at how you're standing in your own way. Here's a different way of seeing yourself and the world that might help you."

In other words, they will help you with subtle shifts in thinking. They will, over time, help you shed the layers of fear that keep you trapped and small and lonely.

What does this look like in daily life? How can we be in constant conversation with our guides and still get our work done?

And, ultimately, what are the benefits? The following is a short list of the many ways—both practical and esoteric—your guides will help you, including some pertinent thoughts from Ella.

They'll be a constant presence.

While we must wait for your requests to help you on specific issues, we are always present to guide and direct, and we are doing this in subtle ways.

For instance, you recall reading a story of guides who were trying to bring two people together so they could start a relationship. These people did not ask specifically for the other. They simply had, somewhere in their unconscious, a thought that they wanted to meet a partner. And so the guides set to work to make it happen. Sometimes the request comes from the contract you set up before you were born. A baby does not ask for our help in the way that you think, and yet we're there attending to that baby. And sometimes other people's prayers can affect what we're able to do for you, whether or not you have consciously asked.

Again, think of a marriage. The spouses support and help one another whether or not they specifically ask for help, do they not? There is always an intention and a backdrop of assisting one another and certainly being there in times of need. You do not direct every movement of one another throughout the day, but you are constantly there in support. And when one of you asks the other for help, you do whatever you can to make it happen. This is very much the same with us.

It is an excellent model for our purposes, because one of the things we want most to do with this book is to demystify the idea of guides and their "superpowers," to relate ourselves more relevantly to souls in human form. We have been there. We know what you're dealing with. If you are about to go flying off the freeway or running headlong into a truck, we will do what we can to prevent it unless it is something you've chosen, even if you do not consciously ask us for help.

They'll expand your creativity.

❥ The combination of your will and ours is unstoppable. The power in it is not fully recognized, except for those who have created great and wondrous things, and even they don't always know how much divine inspiration was behind their inventions.

Here is how it works: In conversation together, either conscious or unconscious, we are feeding information to all of you constantly. There is no exception to this. People's egos will say, "Well, not me. I'm not getting any divine inspiration." Certainly this is true if they have no willingness to listen, but it doesn't mean there is not a flow of information being directed toward them. They simply need to open the portal slightly for the message to get through.

Because of this, you are in a constant state of creativity. People can open up to the creative energy flowing through them from Spirit simply by asking for it to be. Use the prayer, "Please heal my fear-based thoughts so I can open up to divine inspiration and creativity flowing through me." It's that simple. That will start the faucet flowing.

This works for everything . . . no exceptions, once again. The part that the person plays then is not just allowing the energy to come forth, but taking the steps to physicalize it. This is important because it's the part that we can't do without you. This is where you need to listen for our direction. And truly, there is nothing we can't solve.

They'll put what you want right in your path.

A few years ago, my friend Sue decided she was ready to get a new dog after her previous canine companion had died. She wasn't completely sure of making the commitment because she knew the heartache of losing a pet. So she said to Spirit, "If you want me to have another dog, put it right in my path."

A couple of weeks later, she visited a ranch, where she was volunteering with at-risk youth. And there, in the middle of the road, was not one dog, but two. They were adorable. One had short hair and a pointed nose, the other long hair and a fluffy tail. She asked around to see who they belonged to, but no one had seen them before. No collars, no tags. She figured they'd come from a nearby farm.

Two weeks later, she drove back to the same ranch, and there were the same two dogs, again right in her path. Again, everyone she asked knew nothing about them. And so she took them to the shelter, waited a few days to see if anyone claimed them, and then adopted them. Jill and Buddy have been her constant companions ever since. They're like Zen dogs—quiet, well-behaved, perfect for Sue and her life. As usual, the dogs that her guides found for her were better than anything she might have found for herself.

Similarly, an old friend recently found the love of her life when she realized she was ready, after fifteen years of being divorced, to find love again. Just as Sue had done with the dogs, she asked Spirit to put the man she was supposed to be with in her path. And within a few weeks, there he was—a gentleman she'd met before but didn't know well. He was at the grocery store, of all places, and within a week he was actively pursuing her. That was five months ago, and they'll be getting married later this year.

These stories say so many things about partnering with Spirit. First, there's surrender: "I have a desire and don't know how to fill it. But I know you do." Second, there's a request: "Please bring what I'm looking for to me so I don't have to go looking, because I don't know what I'm looking for anyway, and I know what you bring to me will be a thousand times better than I could imagine." And third, there's trust: "I know my job is to have patience and go on with my life, trusting that you will deliver when the timing is perfect."

That's it. It works for everything. It *doesn't* work so well when our egos and our fears get in the way and try to impose a list of criteria and a set schedule. So ask for your fear-based thoughts to be healed, ask to have patience, ask to be as trusting as you can be. Then give thanks for answered prayers.

"

Ask for your

fear-based thoughts

to be healed,

ask to have patience,

ask to be as trusting

as you can be.

"

They'll remind you to be patient.

One of my favorite definitions of patience comes from my friend Dorothy, who always said, "Patience is the ability to witness divine timing, and to do something creative in the meantime."

Your guidance can help you with that.

When *The Only Little Prayer You Need* was released, for instance, I felt compelled to fill up every minute of my day forcing something to happen, and it never felt like enough.

In a morning meditation, I saw a rabbit digging up seeds that hadn't yet sprouted. The message? I was the rabbit. I was trying so hard to *do* something that I was actually interfering with the book's growth. "If you dig up the seeds before they have time to germinate," my guides said, "they can't grow and spread."

I backed off from my ego's need to be in control and waited. A few weeks later, one night when I least expected it, I got the green light. "Now," my guides said, "it's time."

Pay attention when you're pushing out of fear, and ask your guidance for a creative outlet instead.

They'll let you know when it's time for closure.

🐚 We let you know when it's time to move on from a job, a relationship, a home, a friendship, or this lifetime, and you can either accept or resist. Typically, because of the fear receptors, fear is the first response. This limits growth and slows your advancement as you go through life.

Things are not meant to be static and unchanging. You go through the first two decades of your life constantly learning and advancing from one grade level to another. This does not change as you go through the rest of your life, but because you have no defined structure for it, you tend to judge it rather than welcoming it.

You can feel when a situation or person in your life is bringing you sorrow rather than joy. And while there may sometimes be extenuating factors, this is typically a good sign that it's time to make a change in yourself or move on. We can help you define the course of action so you can do so with confidence rather than fear.

They'll serve as your personal lost and found.

My husband Bob recently misplaced notes from one of his construction jobs. It was 9:00 p.m., and he'd last seen them that morning when he thought he took them out to his van. But he'd looked in the van, on his desk, even through the stack of mail, thinking they might have gotten stuck in that pile. Nothing.

"Have you asked your guides?" I said. He sat in his recliner, closed his eyes, and asked them to be specific about where the notes were. A minute later, he opened his eyes and said, "They keep showing me my desk." So he went back to his office and looked again. There they were on his desk, tucked under other papers in a place he'd overlooked.

They'll warn you when you're in jeopardy.

A year or two ago, I woke up on a Saturday morning and had a strong urge to clean out the off-season clothes closet in our basement.

This had never happened before. I can think of about 972 other things I'd typically rather do than clean out that closet, and they include ironing and scrubbing the toilet.

Nevertheless, there was a torrential rain outside, I didn't have anything else pressing on my to-do list, and the urge was strong, as though my guides' hands were on my shoulders, walking me toward the closet. So there I went.

After fifteen minutes or so of sorting through the clothes and making a pile for Goodwill, I saw water on the floor. I looked up, and there, pouring out of the wall at the far end of the closet, was a miniature waterfall. I ran upstairs to tell Bob, and within a few minutes we were mopping up the water and fixing the leak.

If I hadn't been cleaning the closet that morning, the basement likely would have flooded before we discovered it. It made me wonder how many other times the guides have prevented a problem in my life without my ever knowing about it.

They'll assist you whether you know it or not.

Even when you do not feel that you're in touch with your guidance or the relationship is not developing as you think it should, know that you are still being guided. This is important because it allows you to relax and know that the part of your mind that is connected to your guidance is always in operation, even if it is temporarily muddied by fear.

When you focus on what you want, you automatically trip the trigger of your guidance. When you focus on what you do not want, you trip the trigger of fear. So it's important to train your mind and direct your own thoughts to work in harmony with us. This, too, is the meaning of co-creation. It is like choosing a room in which to live. Do you want to live in the room of fear, in which you feel cut off and alone? Or do you want to live in the room of the higher Self and higher thought, in which there are windows that open onto our conversations with

"

Even when you do not feel that you're in touch with your guidance, know that you are still being guided.

"

you, where you can open the window at any time and say, "Let's play!" This is the meaning of co-creation in many ways. As you have a creative thought and we add to it and you are in a place to receive our additions to your thoughts, the creation grows and grows.

This has its roots in ancient stories such as the Bible and other sacred texts, in which the voice of God is speaking to people and waking them up. But it's not just when they're awakened that God has been working with them. God has been there all along, just as we are with you all along.

Sometimes when you're sleeping you will awaken with a start and experience a moment of confusion. "Who am I? Where did I come from? What just happened?" This can indeed be very jarring because there is no instant recognition. It is as if you were sleeping and a stranger came and nudged you awake.

That is why getting to know us can help you, because you will no longer experience those abrupt and sudden moments of introduction.

While this book is about partnering with Spirit and doing so consciously, it is not about doing it a certain way or doing it right to succeed in life. It is simply about expanding your awareness of what's possible for you and being comforted by the fact that we are here with you always, whether you know it or not. Your life will be easier if you speak with us and listen to us openly. But we are helping you either way. That is all.

They'll monitor what you're ready for.

🐟 Spiritual growth can be a bit overwhelming, as though the electrical and physical systems of your body cannot handle the expansion of creativity and thought. And so we are careful not to give you more than you're ready for. People think of that phrase in terms of challenges: God doesn't give you more than you're ready for. But we are also careful in how we introduce you to greater joy, helping you open up to that gradually so it is not too much of a shock to your system. Think of a flower opening to the sun. It unfurls one petal at a time, drinking it in slowly before it becomes fully open and receptive. This is the same with your receptors to us.

We try to make it as easy for you as possible, feeling when you're frightened or overwhelmed or need a break. Your willingness tells us a great deal. We cannot act on your behalf if it would instill more fear in you. This is why changes are often incremental and may seem slower than you would like.

It is important to take good care of your physical body during these times of growth and creation, because you are giving your body new information to which it needs to adjust. Give it healthful food and lots of water and rest. Don't be surprised if your ego tries to shut you down and abandon these conversations with us . . . that is to be expected. While you're talking to us, you may start to yawn or suddenly feel very fatigued. This is both the ego trying to distract you and your body's natural need for more rest as you grow.

Think of an adolescent's growth spurts. There's a reason why teenagers sleep until noon and consume gallons of milk. They need those things to feed their quick growth. Your spiritual growth is similar in that it happens very quickly at times, and you need to be aware of what is happening so you can respond with understanding rather than fear.

They'll pave the way for challenging conversations.

Like any couple, Bob and I don't see eye-to-eye on everything. Some topics, like money and politics, are more filled with landmines than others, but it's impossible to live together without discussing them. So here's an invaluable technique I learned from a healer in Illinois.

Whenever you know you're going to have a potentially contentious conversation, ask your guides to smooth the way ahead of time. Let's say I'm going to talk to Bob about investments. First I ask my guides to open my heart to the conversation—essentially to heal my fear-based thoughts about it. Then I ask them to talk to Bob's guides, who can do the same for him. Bob doesn't even have to know that I've made this request, or that his guides are working with him. But by taking the conversation up to a higher vibration where it can be healed before it even starts, the guides are preparing both of us to speak from love—or at least, neutrality—rather than a posture of attack and defense. It changes the energy before we even walk in the room.

They'll help you forgive.

I have a client who was 19 when her mother was murdered. She's now in her thirties, and because she has worked with Spirit over time, she has been able to forgive the man who committed the crime.

A friend was sexually abused by her grandfather when she was a little girl. With the help of ongoing guidance and healing energy work, she can now claim her own sense of Self and forgive him for the deep void and betrayal she felt all her life.

A woman in one of my classes didn't speak to her brother-in-law for years because of the way he had treated her parents. But when his bull trampled her prized gardens, she realized she was tired of holding on to the anger and asked Spirit for the one thing she wanted most: "Peace in my corner of the world." Before long, she realized her bitterness had simply gone away. She forgave him—and the bull—and the rift in the family has been healed.

We all experience situations, from small annoyances to life-changing violations, that can make forgiveness seem like a noble ideal, but impractical in this world of hurts. One of the most valuable things your spiritual guidance can do is walk with you as you wrestle out of that straitjacket of fear and find the freedom of forgiveness.

It may take time. But when you ask for true forgiveness—not to elevate yourself by taking the high road, but to completely wipe the slate clean of the fear you're hanging on to—you'll set into motion the greatest support system you can imagine. Healing this world of fear will only happen through forgiveness, so when you express a desire to forgive, you're invoking your highest purpose.

Ask for peace in your corner of the world. It's an excellent place to start.

They'll open your spiritual eyes.

There's a beautiful line in *A Course in Miracles* that says, "You have no idea of the tremendous release and deep peace that comes from meeting yourself and your brothers totally without judgment." In other words, when we can see the light rather than fear in ourselves and others, we are healed, and so are they.

Whenever you find yourself in a conflict situation, ask your guides to help you see it from above the battlefield. In other words, view it from your higher Self rather than from your ego. You'll be able to feel the difference. Your ego will want to engage in the conflict and take revenge. Your higher Self will be a neutral and nonjudgmental witness. It may feel like you have a split mind, because you do.

As you collaborate, you begin to see yourself and others the way your guides do. You begin to see beyond the fear to the light within. You start detaching from expectations and outcomes. You begin to meet yourself and others with a desire to extend kindness rather than to control. You see drama for the waste of energy that it is. You can *feel* when you move to the higher Self because you experience the gentle release. And you travel the path of peace and purpose with insights that you never had before.

Meeting Your Guides

It's time to meet your own guides. It's time to begin a relationship that will enhance the rest of your life.

This may seem like a moment that deserves fanfare and ritual. But, in fact, it's very much like saying hello to an old friend. In fact, your guides are eager for you to "pick up the phone" and say hello. And who better to lead you through this simple process than Ella?

It is not difficult to contact your spiritual guidance. In fact, there is probably not a thing that's easier and more natural other than breathing and feeling the beat of your heart.

Unlike human communication, which seems to require some kind of device to span what appears to be distance, there is neither time nor distance involved in your communication with your guides, and no devices are necessary. This is why it seems so unnatural to you, because you have been trained to need tools—a phone that you can pick up, a computer that allows you to see one another. But mental communication—becoming aware of the connections between our minds and yours—requires nothing but your willingness to sit still for a moment and ask.

When you do this, you will find that the world you thought was real has new contours and shape. You'll find that it's without boundaries, and that the veil you never even knew existed because you didn't think about us before simply disappears into the dust and is left behind.

Think of it this way. When you are around a baby, the infant cannot communicate with language, but you still talk to one another, do you not? You and your animal companions communicate even though you are not fluent in one another's languages. And if a stranger from another planet suddenly appeared on your doorstep, you would find a way to create understanding, would you not?

Let me assure you that talking with your guides is easier than all of these examples. The only reason it may seem daunting or illogical or impossible is because we are not in three-dimensional form, and your senses are blocking your ability to see beyond.

But willingness is all it takes to supersede these limitations. You cannot underestimate the power of willingness in your life—not just in communication with us, but in every aspect of what you want to create.

This is what we'd like you to do.

Sit quietly and take several deep breaths. Close your eyes. Feel yourself becoming comfortable and relaxed. If there is any fear in your body, ask for those fear-based thoughts to be healed.

Now see in your mind's eye an invitation. Engraved, handwritten, it can look however you want, but see it clearly. It is an invitation to your guides, stating that you want to communicate with them, inviting them to be part of your life. Bear in mind that they already are attending, but your invitation is a statement to you that you want to feel their presence.

Now see yourself sending that invitation out into the universe, where it will be directed to your guides. Send it out with confidence that it will be received and answered.

Then sit back and wait for the answer to come. Be open to it, in whatever form. Pay attention. When your ego tries to tell you this is silly and you should go make a sandwich or throw in a load of laundry, ask for those fears to be healed and stay right where you are.

Simple, no?

Once you have established this initial communication, build it daily. Do not neglect it. Your guides like to be in conscious contact often and will be there whenever you address us.

As Ella said, it's that simple. I've used this brief visualization with individuals and groups, and it works even for people who are highly skeptical at first.

For Pam, a student in one of my *A Course in Miracles* classes, this visualization had completely unexpected results. She was wary of spirit guides to begin with, but she was willing to go along when I walked the group through this visualization, helping them relax and then instructing them to send an invitation.

She sat with her eyes closed and followed the instructions. As she relaxed more deeply, she found herself aware of three shadows around her—two on her right and one on her left—and began thinking that something might happen after all.

And then, out of the blue, she heard her brother laugh.

He had passed away eight years before, but his laugh was unmistakable to her. He had a specific message for her that night about someone important to her, and she trusted his words. "Here he was," she said, "still poking fun, still teasing, still taking care of me in his own way."

A few weeks later, she had the chance to work with a medium, who confirmed that her brother had been with her. He also said she had two other spirits that weren't coming forward. "The main reason for their unwillingness to do so," he said, "is because you have not attempted to contact them on your own. You must ask to do so before they will agree to speak to me on your behalf."

Since then, she has communicated with those two spirits, who have brought healing and understanding to her during a challenging time.

"I'm becoming a believer," Pam says. "Each of us has spiritual connections should we wish to call upon them and take the chance to believe in them. I'm learning about myself and others that I love, and I have every trust that we're not alone."

How Do You Build a Relationship?

Once you've established contact with your guides, what do you do next? While it's easy to put the guides on a pedestal and believe they're separate from us, that's not true. We're all part of the same whole, and building a relationship with them is essentially the same as cultivating a friendship or partnership with another human being.

After I wrote the chapter about how I met my guides, Ella said the following.

❧ There are key points here that others can learn from. You paid attention. You asked. You were open to a connection. You continued to learn and to concentrate on the relationship. You trusted. These are things anyone can do. You paid attention to small things. You didn't expect the miracles to be grand and dramatic. Slippers, card games . . . you learned early to listen to the ordinary. As in a household where meaning can be conveyed in a hug or a gesture or the most seemingly mundane language of love, you realized that this communication and relationship was the same. You set aside expectations of what it should be and let it be what it was. You were willing. And you believed.

IF YOU THINK BUILDING a relationship with your guides is beyond your ability, or that you have to develop new skills to do it, think again. Here's all you need to get started.

Stand still.

A couple of years ago, a feral cat showed up in our yard—a small gray striped cat who hung around but would run whenever we stepped outside to leave food on the front porch. Before long, we realized this cat was pregnant, and we started calling her Mama Cat. And before too much longer, she gave birth to her kittens in our neighbor's barn.

Over time, we started to win Mama Cat over. I'd be out gardening, and she'd come a little closer each day. I could tell she wanted attention, but she just didn't trust us yet—until one day when she walked right up to me, turned around, stuck her tail up in the air and invited me to scratch her rear end. We've been acquaintances every since.

Mama Cat started bringing her kittens to our house, where she would nurse them on the front porch. But while she became somewhat domesticated, her kittens didn't. They'd run if they even saw us looking at them out the window. Bob built them a shelter that sits on the front porch during the winter, and he rigged up a Wiffle ball tied to a long string that hung from a hook on the front porch, where the kittens could play feline tetherball.

But the kittens continued to run.

One cold day, I felt especially frustrated as I opened the front door to feed them. They were huddled on the porch, but they scattered into the bushes as soon as they heard the door. Their insistence on running every time we reached out to them, their lack of trust that we had their best interest at heart, kept us apart and made their lives harder than they needed to be. So I stood on the front porch in the cold and spoke to them in the bushes.

"If you would just stand still, we could help you."

I thought I was talking to the kittens. But you know how sometimes your words come back to you and smack you in the face? As soon as I said those words, I saw myself surrounded by angels and spirit guides who were pointing at *me* and saying, "If you would just stand still, we could help you."

I realized in that moment how much I, even with all the years of relationship with my guides, still forget to sit down and spend time with them. Like everyone else, I run in circles, trying to find shelter and safety, when the help I need is right there—all around me and *in* me. We run and hide from help rather than accepting it. We run *away* from what we need rather than *toward* it, always out of fear.

So the very first step in building the relationship is simply to stand still. Your guides deserve your full attention, and so do you. Put the multitasking aside, turn off the music, and plant yourself somewhere comfortable for a little while. Come out of the bushes, take a few deep breaths, relax, and go inside.

Find a place that speaks to you.

You can talk to your guides anywhere, but certain places may put you in a more receptive space or may feel more spirit-filled to you. In our house, it's our living room, where the vaulted ceiling and picture windows create a sense of spaciousness.

"

*The very first
step in building
the relationship is
simply to stand still.*

"

Whenever I walk into that room, it feels like I'm entering a quiet space. I have no doubt it's because hundreds of people have sat in that living room for spiritual classes and workshops, not to mention all the gatherings with friends and family. Their combined energies give it a feeling of joy and higher vibration. So when I want to sit and talk with the guides in a space of quiet and reflection, that's where I go. I sit in the rocking chair, close my eyes, breathe in the energy that's all around me, and ask.

Experiment to see if there's a place in your life that speaks to you. Don't use this as a delay tactic or distraction or excuse. Instead, over time, try contacting your guides in different places and see what works best for you.

See yourself as a full partner.

Imagine that you're an employer, and you interview two prospective employees. One walks into your office, head bowed, and says, "I'm lowly and undeserving. I know I'm not good enough, so I understand if you don't want to work with me."

The other walks in, shakes your hand, looks you in the eye and says, "Pleased to meet you. I can bring a lot to this job, and I'm looking forward to what we can accomplish together."

Which one are you going to choose?

You and your guides have already chosen one another, so you don't have to prove yourself to them or justify that you deserve their help. And you also don't have to be falsely humble.

In fact, when you do that, you're affirming the ego's belief that you're undeserving, which makes it hard for anyone (guides included) to give you what you *do* deserve: well-being, prosperity, joy, inner peace, and love.

Whenever you communicate with your guides, show up with confidence, knowing you are greatly loved.

Commit to listening.

Imagine sitting next to a friend who is fully focused on you and is giving you priceless advice. Instead of returning that focus, you're checking for text messages and thinking about the chicken salad you're going to have for lunch. Then you look out the window and say, "Hey, did you see that dog running down the street?"

The friend would likely stand up, leave the room, and not come back.

Thankfully, the guides won't abandon you, but they do want to know that they're being heard and that you value what they're saying. Whether you're meditating, journaling, walking

"

You and your guides have already chosen one another, so you don't have to prove yourself to them or justify that you deserve their help.

"

in the woods, or drawing a picture, practice active listening, ask good questions, and reflect on what they say.

Connect at regular intervals.

Now imagine you're dating someone casually. You talk now and then. And sometimes when he arranges a night out, you reschedule three times or blow it off completely.

Not a good strategy for building a relationship.

In contrast, if you're dating someone you're serious about, you share a sense of momentum and want to spend time together. You get together often, and you value the opportunities to learn more about yourself and one another. You both feel like you're building something that's significant and fulfilling.

That's what you want your relationship with your guides to be. So make a date with them on a regular basis. Talk to them daily, even if it's only for a couple of minutes. Set aside a regular time: ten minutes as soon as you wake up in the morning or five minutes at lunch. Be dependable. Show up. If they can't count on you, you're only slowing your own path to growth and greater happiness.

Be a joyful receiver.

Think of it this way: Your husband gives you a bouquet of tulips and your response is, "Hmmm, was the florist out of roses?" Or someone gives you a million dollars and you shrug and say, "Well, it's a start." Or a friend sends you a gift card through the mail and you keep forgetting to acknowledge that you got it.

You may stop receiving presents before too long.

But imagine this: You give your young niece a gift for Christmas, and her face is aglow with excitement and appreciation when she opens it. And even though you didn't have to wrestle it out of the hands of five other people at 12:01 a.m. on Black Friday, she still says, "This is the best gift I've ever gotten!" Well, you can be pretty sure you'll be shopping for her again and again.

Your guides need your appreciation and acknowledgement. On some level, I'm sure there are entities that are beyond the need for gratitude. But spirit guides in general still appreciate being appreciated. Don't fake it. Just know that everything they give you is a treasure. Receive graciously.

Appreciate their humor.

I did a morning meditation last year on March 4, and when my guides signed off they said, "*March forth* with clarity and know that all is well." Very clever. Pay attention. They'll surprise you with their playfulness.

Be decisive.

Let's say you've told some friends you want to buy a house, so they start looking online for you. They send you some listings and text you when they drive by a place they think is just your style.

But then you back off and say, "Well, I'm not sure. I don't know if it's the right time to move."

So the friends unsubscribe to the real estate listing services.

Two days later you tell them, "Yep, I've decided. I definitely want to move."

And they start looking on your behalf again.

A week later, you come back and say, again, "Well, I don't know . . ."

Exhausting, isn't it?

Even if you're a spiritual guide with unlimited resources available, it's almost impossible to help someone who keeps changing their mind.

This doesn't mean we always have to know what we want. In fact, part of what the guides do so well is helping us to identify and claim what would make us truly joyful.

But when you and your guides *do* know, and you keep backing off from it out of fear, you're setting up a hair-pulling situation for entities that probably don't even *have* hair.

A recent example: We were invited to go on vacation, agreed that we wanted to go, and then sank into confusion. *Should we spend the money? Can we afford the time? Who will take care of the cats? What if there's a storm while we're gone and a tree falls on our roof and our neighbors have suddenly decided to go to Tahiti so no one knows that our house is filling up with water, inch by inch?*

The guides' response?

"First of all," they told me, "ask for your fear-based thoughts to be healed about all of *that*. And second," they said, "if you want to go, go. We'll take care of the details."

Oh, yeah. They can do that. Line up the money, arrange for the time, and direct storms around our house if they have to. We booked the tickets that afternoon.

Trust them. They're your *team*.

Focus on your own soul growth.

One of the ego's greatest tricks is to distract you from your own inner growth by pointing out what everyone else—including

"

It's time to stop worrying about that which you do not understand, cannot see, and are not responsible for.

"

adult children, colleagues, best friends, and distant cousins—"should" be doing to live a more successful or happier life. Trust me, the guides don't have a lot of patience for this.

One day when Bob had been listening to talk radio and was in a "the sky is falling" mode, I started to focus on *his* fears rather than my own. That's when I heard my guides say, "Leave him alone. This is important for his soul growth."

Got it. He has his *own* path to follow. I forgot.

A couple of days later, I looked out our back window at some spruce trees that were once stately but had suffered from blight. Spraying and pruning hadn't helped, and neither had my efforts to control their future. "Their growth and healing," I heard my guides say, "is between them and God."

Right again.

Not long after, I was stewing about a business decision that was not mine to make, and I heard my guides again loud and clear:

"It's time to stop worrying about that which you do not understand, cannot see, and are not responsible for."

Alrighty then. This is why they deserve their own book.

The more you focus on building your relationship with your guides, the more you'll realize that other people's issues—just like the spruce trees—are between them and a higher power, not between them and you. It's astonishing how much easier life becomes when we're not mentally meddling in everybody else's business. The guides have little time for virtual gossip. Their ability to bring you back to your Self is one of their greatest gifts.

A Day in the Life with Your Guides

There's a phrase we use a lot around our house: "Thank you to the guides."

When Bob comes home from a building project and tells me about a near miss with a power tool, my immediate response is, "Thank you to the guides."

When our rental van is sideswiped on vacation, no one is hurt, and I remember that Spirit can turn a potential headache into a minor inconvenience: "Thank you to the guides."

When I have a meeting scheduled but feel pinched for time and the *other* party texts me to reschedule: "Thank you to the guides."

I think it's worth mentioning again that this is how it looks and sounds for me. You may express gratitude to God, Jesus,

"

Thank you

to the

guides.

"

the Holy Spirit, an archangel, or another divine being. Or you may feel blessed by a nameless positive energy that flows through you and gives you a heightened sense of awareness.

This energy all flows from the same Source, so no matter what it looks and feels like to you, the point is to be mindful of it daily, and to work with it intentionally.

This means sitting down, letting your breathing slow, and paying attention. There is no secret or magic to this. It begins by aligning your thoughts with love and guidance, whatever form that will take for you.

Sometimes, though, it helps to get a concrete picture. With that in mind, here are some specific ways that you can spend your day with your own guidance.

- Before you get out of bed, acknowledge your guidance and give thanks for it. Reflect on the kind of day you'd like to have. Detach from anything that might induce anxiety, and ask for a day of peace and purpose.

- Ask what you can do for the guides today.

- Ask them to remind you of anything you need to remember throughout the day, and to give you the words to say that will serve the highest good in any situation.

❧ In the first ten minutes that you're up, look for three beautiful things in your environment and the other people in your household. With each one, take at least twenty seconds to notice, admire, and give thanks.

❧ As you get everyone up and out the door for the morning, add a few mindfulness rituals to your routine. While you're brushing your teeth, ask your guides a question. As you're drying your hair, ask for your fear-based thoughts to be healed. As you're packing the kids' lunches, give thanks once again.

❧ When you get in the car, thank the guides for safe travels.

❧ Sometime during your morning, spend five minutes in prayer or meditation. Ask your guides a specific question that's on your mind.

❧ Whenever you need to make a decision, ask your guides what will serve the highest good of all.

"

Whenever you need to make a decision, ask your guides what will serve the highest good of all.

"

When your ego resists their answer, ask for your fear-based thoughts to be healed.

❧ During your lunch hour, spend five minutes noting or writing about the abundance you experience in your life. Document something different each day: an abundance of joy, creativity, fun, love, family, money, freedom, adventure, etc.

❧ Whenever a challenge or something worrisome comes up, turn first to your guides and ask for their help so you can feel an immediate comfort. This will help prevent your ego from ramping up and making the situation worse out of fear.

❧ All day long, notice serendipitous events and thank your guides for orchestrating your life with so much creativity and loving attention to detail.

❧ Before you go to bed, look back over your day and notice or write about three things that gave you special joy or satisfaction. Thank the guides for their role in making those things possible.

❧ Before you go to sleep, pose a question to your guides and ask for them to communicate with you in your dreams. If you want to wake up with an answer to a specific question, let them know.

As you can see, these kinds of communications can happen with no disruption to your routine and without any special preparation. Over time, you'll find yourself conversing with your guides constantly through the day.

Sometimes, though, you'll want an even deeper conversation, especially if you're wrestling with an issue in your life or you're confused about why something is happening. At those times, I highly recommend setting aside twenty to thirty minutes and sitting quietly with a pen and paper so you can jot down key insights or record your guidance directly.

Then, simply ask questions that will get to the heart of whatever is on your mind.

- ❧ What would help me grow right now?

- ❧ What do I need to focus on?

- ❧ What do I need to know in this moment?

- ❧ What's holding me back?

- ❧ What do I need to let go of?

- ❧ How can I find the love I'm looking for?

"

What would

help me grow

right now?

"

- How can I have a more loving relationship with my partner?

- What are my strengths as a parent? How can I be a better parent?

- How can I talk with the people in my life so we can come to greater understanding?

- How can I be more forgiving?

- Who do I need to forgive?

- Why am I having such a hard time loving myself?

- How can I take better care of myself?

- How can I be more compassionate?

- How can I disagree without getting angry?

- What am I here for?

- What do I really want?

- What fears are standing in my way right now?

- Why do I make things hard?

- How can I stop fighting myself?

"

*What fears are
standing in my way
right now?*

"

Approach these conversations exactly the way you would if there were another being sitting next to you, because there is. You have no idea how rich, fulfilling, growthful, and life-changing these conversations will be—and not just for you. Your guides will celebrate this growing relationship right along with you.

As soon as you have an *aha* moment in these conversations—and you will—know that you've experienced a miracle. You're forever changed. The shift in you has already happened, just like it did for me the night I was sixteen and won those five solitaire games.

At that point, you can bet your ego is going to march into your line of sight, stamp its foot, say *Enough!*, and try to distract you with a rerun of *America's Got Talent* or a plate of lemon bars. But you can't go back. You can never *not* know what you now know about yourself.

These regular conversations will fortify you. They'll help you stand taller in the grandeur of your spiritual strength. They'll allow you to pat the ego on the head, give it a popsicle, and send it off to play.

"We Don't Have to Help You"

Throughout this book, I've emphasized that the relationship with your guides is equivalent in many ways to your relationships with other people. I've also said how important it is to express your gratitude daily. But these two points are so important, I want to drive them home by sharing a not-so-comfortable experience of mine from a few years ago, when I had a major meltdown about money.

Actually, it wasn't just about money. It was about feeling that I wasn't progressing in my career the way I wanted to. I was taking on projects I didn't want to do because they paid the bills, but they didn't give me any joy or satisfaction. I was helping others move forward with their writing but wasn't doing the same for myself. And, as my guides so succinctly pointed out to me one day, "Trying to get published without writing is like trying to get pregnant without having sex."

Point taken.

My feelings came to a head one day when one of my writing clients had an op/ed piece published in the *Washington Post*. The *Washington Post*! She sent it in one day, and it was published the next.

And so my meltdown began.

Was I happy for her? Sure. Was I jealous and internally screaming *What about me?* Definitely.

And then I did something I'd never done before. I blamed it all on my guides.

Typically, in that kind of situation, I would have asked my guides what I could learn from it, what lesson it held for me, what I could do differently from that point on. But this time, years of frustration exploded in finger-pointing and the loudest, most fear-driven blame I could think of, all directed at my team.

"You're not helping me," I yelled. I literally yelled out loud, "I'm doing everything I possibly can, and you're not supporting me."

That was nasty enough, but it got *much* worse from there. It was so bad that, when I told one of my best friends about it with all the vehemence I was feeling, she literally drew back and stared at me, frightened. "Who *are* you?" she said.

She didn't need to be scared, because I had more than enough fear for the entire state of Iowa. And the only ones I wanted to hurt in that moment were my guides, those beings of light in white jogging suits who had been cheering me on. It was one of the biggest ego tantrums and explosions I've ever experienced, and I kept at it, righteously holding on to my anger and indignation for two days.

Ugly doesn't begin to describe it.

Gradually, I settled down, but my ego refused to give in. I talked to my guides, but I was still angry with them, believing they were somehow standing in the way of the flow of money I thought I deserved. But over time, I started to behave with a bit more sanity.

Fast forward three months.

I was on the phone with a healer in Illinois, a woman who specializes in working with entities. I was talking to my guides through her, asking questions and receiving their responses. I asked about my writing, and they gave me excellent, practical advice.

Then I asked about money. She posed the question to Ralph, the name I'd given my primary guide, and there was silence on the phone.

"Hmm," she finally said, "I've never heard a guide say this before."

She, of course, knew nothing about my tirade against the guides. She said, "Let me ask again."

Again, silence.

Then she said, "Well, this surprises me, but he's saying he doesn't have to help you with money because you're ungrateful."

Oops. I immediately thought of my tantrum a few months earlier.

I gulped. "Really?" I said, feeling suddenly chastened. "Does he say anything else about it?"

She checked in. "He's saying that they help you all the time, but you don't acknowledge it."

I took a deep breath, realized I'd been busted, and told her the story of blaming my guides. She listened and then said, "Well, I think you need to apologize."

And so I did. I took responsibility, asked for their forgiveness, and thanked them for the countless ways—so many of which are unknown to me—that they help me every single day.

And I haven't blamed them for anything since.

The experience was painful, but it taught me an enormous lesson. Until that time, I figured guides were higher

"

Recognize their devotion to you, and that they will do everything in their power to help.

"

beings beyond human emotion, available to serve us in any way we asked. But their response to my behavior was exactly the same as if I'd mistreated another human being. They are not interested in being taken advantage of, abused, or blamed. They want to be acknowledged and appreciated for the work they do.

This is so important.

For the non-physical souls who work with us daily, kindness matters. So does appreciation, respect, listening, and generosity.

So here are a few important tips, which I learned the hard way:

- ❧ When you ask for something, trust that they are doing everything possible to bring it your way.

- ❧ When they give you direction, follow it.

- ❧ When you don't understand, ask questions and listen rather than arguing or insisting that you're right.

- ❧ When you set a time to meet with them, be on time.

- Recognize their devotion to you, and that they will do everything in their power to help.

- Most of all, give thanks daily for everything they do on your behalf. Believe me, they deserve it.

Spiritual Blackout

I'm in a spiritual blackout right now, and it's not pretty.

Typically I feel like I have an open line of conversation with spiritual guidance. It's as though there's a phone line extending from my right temple, just above the eye, to some unnamed place in the ether. It feels like my guides are with and around me, close by, always available, and we can chat throughout the day, whenever I need help and remember to ask for it.

And then the spiritual blackout comes along. Wham! Someone shuts a trapdoor overhead, cutting the phone line, and everything goes dark. It's the dark night of the soul, the wandering in the wilderness. It's not just a bad mood, irritability, or frustration. This is a full-fledged, fear-driven fury of silence and sadness.

"

This is a full-fledged, fear-driven fury of silence and sadness.

"

Even while I'm in it, I know a lot of things. I know my guides are still right here and communicating with me, but my fear has created such a barrier that I can't hear them, or I choose not to because my ego has taken me hostage.

I know that I'm miserable and that I don't have to feel this way, but I'm choosing on some level to wallow in it.

I know that the trapdoor will open and the lights will go on again.

I know that something—an *aha* moment, an insight, or a sense of greater strength—will come out of this.

I know that the spiritual blackouts are fewer and farther between, and I also know that this one won't be the last.

Blackouts are tricky because they can be initiated by all sorts of things, leading us to believe that the problem is the trigger, not what's inside us. But it's essential to know that the blackout is always caused by your own fear, not by whatever triggered the fear. Your ego will want to blame it on someone, but that's just a distraction.

For instance, the first-class blackout I'm in right now began after I vacationed with six other people for more than a week. As a classic introvert, I need alone time to recharge my batteries, and I didn't have any for almost ten days. It was as though my spiritual immune system was compromised, and fear came

"

Your ego will want to blame it on someone, but that's just a distraction.

"

in and took over. The people I vacationed with didn't cause it. I just ignored my own needs.

And now, my ego is unrelenting. I know that all of this will be much better in a few days. But, man, is it an awful place to be while I'm there.

This is how I feel during a spiritual blackout: Everything is broken, and nothing will ever be right again. I blame everyone else for my problems, or I blame myself. I feel like I don't deserve happiness, abundance, or love. I've messed up everything, made stupid mistakes, and I deserve to be punished with the misery I'm feeling. There is no one who can help me. Words of encouragement or comfort simply bounce off me because I don't feel I deserve them. Happy people are annoying or, worse, a threat. I'm hypersensitive and can start to cry easily. There is nothing good in the world, and it's only going to get worse. I have feelings of "What's the use?" and wonder if I shouldn't walk away from everything. I feel like all the energy has drained out of me, and I'm susceptible to getting sick.

It's like being a trapped animal desperately seeking an escape and believing there isn't any. In extreme cases, I understand why this can lead to suicide or violence. It is a profound forgetting of who we are, a suppression of light so complete that no resolution seems possible. It is fear, through and through.

In my mind, grief and depression are forms of spiritual blackout. I remember reading a letter my grandfather wrote to my dad after one of my dad's brothers passed away at the age of twelve. "Will attempt to scribble a few lines to you," my grandfather wrote. "In so doing will have my mind occupied with something pleasant for a short while, at least. Everything is dark and gloomy to me and I suppose always will be the rest of my short stay here."

That's the feeling—that life will never be good again. With grief, there's often an accompanying guilt that *If I had only done something, I could have prevented the loss. I could have saved them.* This can lead to a great, deep darkness that may persist, as my grandfather believed it would.

But remember this: It's possible to be discouraged, feeling a lack of courage in facing another day. It's possible to be disheartened, as though your heart is closed to giving or receiving love.

But it's not possible to be truly dispirited, because no matter how black the darkness may seem, your spirit and the light of your guides shine on through it all.

Be gentle with yourself. Know that help is available to you always.

"

Be gentle with yourself. Know that help is available to you always.

"

And remember that whenever you have a spiritual blackout, there will be a reward of inner growth and greater peace once you can feel the sun on your face again.

Ella, what do you have to say about spiritual blackouts?

Thank you for asking. This is what I want your readers to know: spiritual blackouts are necessary and helpful. Just as plants need dormancy and darkness, so do the soul and the mind. A blackout is a rest period, even though it can feel unrestful. The only reason it feels that way is because you resist and fight it and there is so much fear around it. Stop judging it and you will not be so miserable. It is a time to rest and rejuvenate and nourish yourself, as you know, but this is on a different level.

Your electrical system is expanding, and often the blackout is caused by on overloaded circuit. A blackout is the perfect name for it, because it's as though the fuses have been blown, and there needs to be a period of rest before the lights go back on. This is why your pleas for help seem to go unbidden, because it's simply not time yet. You need to be quiet and under the radar, if you will. Because you expect to feel good all the time, though, you judge the experience and think something is wrong with you. Instead, embrace the times of darkness and get lots of sleep and be quiet, and you will grow more quickly once the light shines again.

There is nothing wrong with spiritual blackouts because, as you say, they can lead to great growth. But the misery in them can be minimized if you work with them rather than against them. Growth is inevitable. Misery is optional.

It is important to make the point that our availability to you does not change during this time. In fact, we hover close and are protective because we understand how awful you feel while you're in the darkness. We are here with you always, whether you are aware or can hear us or not.

So what do you do when praying doesn't seem to help, when you are committed to the misery? How can you be sure that the dark night will end, or that you want it to? When you don't know anything else is available to you, what do you do?

There can be a feeling of desperation in spiritual blackout, a giving up. It's important to know that there are two ways to give up. One is giving up control, which is an act of the higher Self—a statement of trust in a higher power. It is giving up trying so hard. Giving up the fight. The other is giving up hope, which is an act of the ego—a statement of fear that you're not good enough to deserve happiness.

This is when you use prayer not as a request, but as a lifeline. You use it even when you don't believe it's being heard. You recognize the fear, and that the prison you seem to be in is only of your own mind. We can help you, but only if you ask. "Please heal my fear-based thoughts even though I don't feel like I deserve it." "Please heal my fear-based thoughts even though I don't think it will help." "Please heal my commitment to fear in this moment so I can remember the light that I am."

Then take a nap. Go for a walk. Sit and cry. Beat on a pillow. Reach out to someone. Write out your misery. Do whatever productive thing you can to expel the fear from your body, which will help accelerate the healing. Most of all, remember that this darkness is not you. It is a belief system that has taken hold temporarily but will loosen its grip so you can remember the light that you are. And remember, we are here with you always. Ask us for help.

The blackout may seem like a long road for some people, other times it will be short—a matter of hours or days. So the most important thing, no matter what the duration, is to remember that the light within you is still shining through it all. You may not see or feel it. It may feel like the pilot light has been snuffed out. But that is not possible. Hold on to that light, no matter how dim it may seem, because it is not shining any less than usual. It's just that you've heaped more fear on it and have made it seem less powerful.

*What you might say to say to your guides
when you're in a blackout.*

I have fallen asleep. I know this is temporary, but it makes me feel cut off from you and alone.

I know this is just my ego talking, but it feels very real. I know this is not who I am. It is just a spiritual blackout that makes me feel like I can't talk to you and receive your guidance like I usually do.

My ego wants me to believe I've messed up and made mistakes that can't be fixed. But I know these are just errors in my thinking and that you can correct them. I ask for your help as I go through this time. Please help me wake up with new insights. This will yield something wonderful if I pay attention and look for the gift.

Thank you for your constant presence and comfort, even when I'm not able to fully and consciously receive.

Peace and Purpose

In Betty Eady's classic book *Embraced by the Light*, she describes a near-death experience in which she was accompanied by spirit escorts who showed her the Earth from a perspective of love rather than fear. One scene from that book has always stayed with me. In fact, I hadn't read the book for years, but I wanted to include a reference to this particular story. I recently went to the bookcase, pulled the book off the shelf, and opened right to the chapter that included the scene I was looking for.

Thank you to the guides.

In this chapter, Betty is shown a drunken man lying on the sidewalk on a city street. Her spirit escorts ask her what she sees and she replies, "A drunken bum lying in his wallow."

Her escorts then show her who he really is, and she sees a man who is filled with light and admired on the other side.

He had taken on the role of a drunk, the escorts told Betty, to help another soul, an attorney. Whenever the attorney saw him, he would be prompted to do more good in this life. The drunken man was fulfilling his chosen role even though, by all appearances, he was someone people would judge as unworthy of their time.

Here's the point: whoever you are and whatever you think of yourself, on a soul level you are a teacher of God, love, and truth.

Co-creating with Spirit helps you remember who you are and what you're here for beyond your ego, your fear, and your personality.

You have a mission or purpose in this life. It may seem to elude you because so often we define our purpose as a job or an achievement. We measure our success by numbers—the likes on Facebook or figures in our bank accounts—rather than the kindness and compassion our actions inspire in ourselves and others.

You may never know your purpose completely while you're here, but by co-creating with your guides and getting to know yourself on a deeper level, you can become clearer about what it is and stay true to it more easily.

"

Here's the point:
whoever you are and
whatever you think of
yourself, on a soul level
you are a teacher of God,
love, and truth.

"

Your mission might be to comfort someone who has experienced loss, or to bring light to a workplace, or to show others how to laugh. You may be here to help one person or to help thousands. But one thing is certain, if you show up with kindness and compassion wherever you go, you'll fulfill your purpose whether you know it or not.

How can the practice of turning inside for answers help you access information that's not available to you in the outside world? How can it help you understand who you are beyond your personality? How can it help you freely express all of who you are? How can it help you manifest what you want most in life? Let me tell you a story abut how it happened for me.

TWENTY-FIVE YEARS AGO, I saw the Lady in the Blue Dress for the first time.

I was lying in bed, on the verge of sleep, when she suddenly appeared in my mind's eye. She was just *there*, sitting on a barstool in a cobalt blue strapless cocktail dress. She looked vaguely familiar, but I couldn't place her. She looked about my age, with shoulder-length auburn hair and a great figure. She was sitting cross-legged on a bar stool and leaning on a counter, but she wasn't in a bar. She wasn't anywhere in particular, really. All I saw was *her*, inside and out. In that flash, I not only saw what she looked like . . . I knew her. I knew that she was no-nonsense. Absolutely clear. She wasn't boastful or egotistical, just exactly who she was. She saw self-doubt as a waste of time. I was taken by her attitude, which was not cocky, but clearly sent a message of "Don't mess with me, because I know who I am."

Her presence caught me by surprise, and my first reaction was to ask, "Who was that?"

The answer, which came back as clearly as the color of her dress, would have knocked me over if I weren't already lying down.

"It's you," my guides said. "The truth of who you are."

This seemed a little too far-fetched for even me to believe. First of all, I would never look like that in a strapless dress. Second, I would never look like that in a strapless dress. And third, I would never look like that in a strapless dress.

Oh, and the self-doubt thing? I had tons of it. Self-doubt was the guiding light of my life, supported by a long list of dos and don'ts. Do be wishy-washy. Do be nice so people will like you. Do sacrifice yourself to the needs of others. Don't do anything that might cause disapproval or conflict. Don't be too sensuous. And don't, above all else, be impolite. You are a midwesterner, after all.

Seeing the Lady in the Blue Dress was like looking in the mirror, but not recognizing the reflection looking back. She had seen me with complete knowing. Maybe that was the spookiest part. I realized she was wise, knew it, and trusted herself completely. And, against all the rules, she wasn't trying to hide it.

I started talking to her. I'd be in the kitchen, mixing up tuna salad for a sandwich and going over a freelance writing assignment in my mind, saying out loud, "Okay, you could take on this job, even though you swore off writing newsletters years ago. But the company is good, the money would be nice, I don't want to upset anyone, I want everyone to like me . . ." My conversation with myself would deteriorate into the equivalent of "blah, blah, blah, blah, blah."

Then I'd ask the Lady, "Should I take the assignment?"

"No," she'd say. Just like that. No hesitation. No agonizing. She just knew. Over time, it dawned on me that this could be a real asset. If I ever needed a new car, she was the one I'd send into the sales office to negotiate. If I were on a date and a man slighted me, well, watch out. She was the Unsinkable Molly Brown of my soul, with Jane Austen's reserve and Oprah's sense of self. She became my ballast, my compass, and my guide.

"Do you know what's going to happen in my life?" I asked her, wondering if she could give me some relationship advice.

"It's a secret," she said, "but I can tell you that you'll be happy. You can't lose."

"Cool," I said. "You're pretty cool."

"It's about time you gave me some credit," she said.

Over time, I developed a routine with the Lady in the Blue Dress. Every few weeks—whenever I felt a need to check in—I did a visualization in which I saw myself walking up to her front door and visiting her at her house. This may sound a little mind-bending—seeing myself being greeted by a higher version of me. But it gave me a chance to see who I was without the fears and façades of my own personality.

On the first visit, I noticed that her screen door had a rip in it, and I immediately thought, "The woman who lives here deserves to have a screen in good repair."

Oh, I realized. That's me. I took the door to the hardware store to be repaired later that week.

With every visit, I absorbed more of her clarity and confidence. She was unshakeable, unfettered by fear.

And then it really got good.

At this point in my life, I'd been divorced for fifteen years, and I'd created a whole string of unsatisfying relationships. I'd reached a point where I felt my life was confining, as though I'd gone as far as I could on my own. To fulfill a larger purpose, I needed a partner. Clearly, though, I had no idea how to find him.

While on a writing retreat, I decided to go see the Lady in the Blue Dress since I hadn't visited her in a while. What would I see when I came to her front door? What would her life look like now?

I took a deep breath, asked my guides for their assistance, and closed my eyes. In my mind's eye, I was standing on the Lady's front porch once again, looking inside. I would write everything I experienced, I decided, acting simultaneously as a witness and a reporter. So I opened my eyes halfway and began to note my observations.

Clean, uncluttered, simple house. The peace of simplicity. Tranquility, acceptance, assurance. Nothing needs to be hard. No apologies for anything. No angst. No judgment. Flowers everywhere. Iced tea or water with lemon in pretty glasses.

In contrast to my house in real life, hers was in order. That part was similar to what I'd seen before. But she was about to show me something new.

"Here's my latest book," she offers—she has them on the coffee table. No big deal about them. Proud, not insecure or egotistical.

*Can't imagine her working. Like the books just manifest them-
selves because why make it hard? This is what needs to be said,
say it and move on.*

As I wrote, I could feel myself slipping into this house,
this attitude, this body of the Lady. But how, I asked, does the
Lady do when she goes out into the world?

"As she moves through her day, she notices the beauty
wherever she looks and takes it into her heart so that each
moment becomes a prayer."

I liked that part. Each moment becomes a prayer.

As I talked to the Lady, her surroundings seemed familiar
and reassuring. Then, from the edge of the scene in my mind's
eye, someone new appeared.

---

*Man walks up behind her and rubs her shoulders. His energy is
as big and calm as hers. He is not subservient or trying to impress
her, but he is the one who takes care of her. She takes his hand
and says so.*

Whoa. I had never seen the Lady with a partner before. She
had always been alone, independent, self-sufficient. With this
man, she maintained her sense of self, yet was sharing it with
another. I couldn't see his face but I could see that he was dressed

all in black, and his energy was steady and comforting, as unique as a fingerprint. Surprised, I asked for more information.

My mind was led back to my ex-husband, whom I had divorced fifteen years earlier. I had wanted to meet someone my junior year of college, get engaged my senior year, and marry after graduation. That's exactly what had happened. Unfortunately, I had failed to ask that he and I love and support each other, too. I had asked for a schedule, not a marriage partner.

Then I thought about the Lady and the man standing behind her, rubbing her shoulders. He had a presence, a sense of strength and devotion that didn't compromise his own needs. He was tall and slender, with dark hair. This is what I recorded, a prayer to a higher power and to my guides:

I now ask, with complete knowing that Your will be done, for a spiritual partner to manifest in my life. I ask that he have the energy I felt in this visit with the Lady—strong, self-assured, supportive, spiritual. A strong soul in his own right, yet happy to be supportive of my needs. I ask that he be kind, gentle, and loving, that he be my best friend, that we have a great chemistry and passion, and that we have a shared mission in the world while fully respecting one another's individual passions. I ask that he be attractive and fun, and that he bring out the best in me. Finally, I ask that he manifest in the normal course of my life, without my seeking him out in any way. And I ask that you let me be the right partner for him as well. And so it is. Thank you.

I felt a sense of completion, but still a nagging fear. After all the years of saying I wanted a partner, was I being honest with myself? I wanted my ex-husband out of fear of being alone. Why did I want a spiritual partner?

For expansion. To multiply love, happiness, peace, and joy by sharing it in the intimacy of daily life. And it wouldn't hurt to get the lawn mowed once in a while.

Even though I didn't realize it at the time, I had reached the point of readiness for a life partner. All the restlessness I'd been feeling in previous months was a reminder from my guides that I'd outgrown my life as it was. To keep moving forward, I needed support. And that meant surrendering my need for control to a higher purpose.

Five weeks later, my guides arranged for me to attend a barn dance—a place I'd never been and didn't want to be. There, across the barn, stood a tall, slender man who seemed familiar, even though I'd never met him. Before long, we were dancing together to the sound of the fiddle and banjo music.

"

Your capacity to know and understand yourself may be the most important byproduct of partnering with your guides.

"

It was funny, but every time I stood next to him, I wanted to lean into him. At first I didn't know why, until my guides reminded me: the energy I felt from him was the energy of the man I'd seen with the Lady in the Blue Dress.

We got married one year later.

YOUR CAPACITY TO KNOW and understand yourself—to see yourself from new perspectives, even to see into your own future—may be the most important byproduct of partnering with your guides.

You don't have to do a particular kind of visualization or follow any specific path to get to know yourself with your guides' help. But over time, you'll notice some basic shifts.

You'll stop sabotaging yourself so you can claim joy.

You'll make decisions that will help you move forward faster in your life.

You'll rely more on Spirit and less on ego.

You'll remember that you are more than your job or your house or your relationships.

You'll understand that the manifestation of your desires goes hand in hand with your purpose.

And you'll know that, with divine timing and the guidance of your unseen helpers, you'll fulfill that purpose in ways that will serve you beyond your greatest imagination.

Key Lessons from the Guides

It could take me the rest of my life to write everything I've learned from my guides because new lessons show up daily. But here are some of the key *aha* moments that I would never have had without my partnership with them, all in the guides' own words.

My reason for including these teachings is twofold: first, to share information that I believe will help you function more efficiently and happily, and second, to illustrate the depth of learning that's possible when you communicate with your guides on a regular basis. In my experience, these are not the kinds of conversations you'll have very often with other humans. And even if you do, there's something about direct coaching from your guides that sends it straight to your soul, where instant change is possible.

Don't take my word for it about these topics, though. Ask your guides about them and see what they tell you.

Be fully human and fully divine.

This is the topic I would like to introduce: how to find the meaning in everyday things with the help of your spiritual guidance. We have not really addressed that of yet, and it is an important part of the experience we're writing about. Is this agreeable to you?

Very well. What I want to get across is this: From the beginning of time, humans have had a deep link and association to the land and physical environment around them. Humans are reliant on the earth and the sky and the heavens and plants and animals for their very existence, yet that link and bond with the environment is suffering greatly, as so many of you are very unaware of the role it plays in your subsistence.

One of the reasons it's important to have a relationship with your spiritual guidance is to remember and honor the world around you. This may seem odd, when spiritual guidance is focused on the unseen, the non-physical. Yet the whole point of our relationship is to help you grow spiritually and extend more love into this physical world. We work with you so that you can become more comfortable in your own skin and in this physical existence, while at the same time remembering that your physical existence does not define who

"

There is not one place better than another, for every place is suited to your growth.

"

you are. It is a conundrum and seems like a contradiction, but I can assure you it is not.

One of the things we want you to do is to become mindful. This is why we ask you to sit and breathe deeply and listen carefully, because it is so easy otherwise to miss your entire life. As people open up to working with their guides and slowing down and paying attention to them, they will also slow down and pay attention to the environment in which they live. This is not a political message about the decline of the Earth's resources. It is instead a reminder that this physical world is a place of wonder and creativity, and if you forget to pay attention to the trees and rivers and mountains, you will miss much of the appeal of coming into this human life.

There are wondrous things around you every day, whether you live on a farm in the middle of your country or you live in a high rise in Beijing. There is not one place better than another, for every place is suited to your growth. And you can learn and strengthen your spirit wherever you are. The key is to pay attention wherever you are, and this is how we can help you.

Think of all the ways we have led you to become more aware of your environment. By taking walks in which you look for something different in nature each time. By walking the perimeter of your land and singing a chant of healing. By becoming aware of the rhythm of the seasons and the natural crescendo and denouement of each day. These are not random acts that you are doing by accident. This is with small touches and reminders that help you remember to open your eyes and see the lushness around you.

We want each and every reader and each practitioner of these words to take time to remember the specialness of the place in which you live. We're not talking about the four walls you inhabit right now, although that is fine too. But the bigger environment. The planet that sustains you, the food that comes from the land that nourishes you. The tea and coffee you drink that grow on hillsides.

Whether you remember it or not, you are rooted to the land by your very existence, and it is important to nourish and replenish this bond from time to time, even if you live in a bustling city where natural beauty is hard to come by. Even if there is no grass, you can admire the clouds and the sky. Even if there are no trees, you can give thanks for the water flowing out of your faucet.

Why is it important to do these things in terms of our relationship with you? Because they anchor you to your physical form and fill up your cells with memories of your physical heritage. We are here to help you bring heaven to earth. If you are not grounded to the earth, our messages and assistance are truncated. They cannot travel to their final destination. The energy is left without a grounding wire to complete it.

Be fully physical even as you are fully spiritual. This is the best and most effective and complete way to bring the energy of the heavens into your being and to be the vessel that will carry it into the world.

Here are things your readers might do to make this happen.

Eat more greens. Do it not just because it will help you maintain a better weight and fill your cells with vitamins, but because it will feed you the very essence of what grows from the earth in its purest form.

Climb trees, or hug them, or sit under them. Let them shelter and protect you. Eat from them, admire their beauty. They bring far more to your existence than you realize. The world would not be possible without them.

Honor the animals around you. Birds, insects, pets, animal companions . . . whatever and wherever they may be, they each have a message for you. There is not one that comes into your life randomly. Give thanks for them. Share your life with them.

Look into the sky every day. Study the clouds and the stars. Honor the miracle of rain. Give thanks for the sun. Remember that you are where you are at the pleasure of these elements that work together to sustain you. You cannot be separate from them, just as we cannot be separate from you.

These simple acts will bring more kindness to your heart and alleviate the stress you often carry there. They are a reminder that everything is working together to support you and that you can expect this from our relationship as well.

Go now and take a walk.

We love you and honor you. All is well.

Use thoughts as building blocks.

❧ Thought seems ephemeral and random. From your human vantage point, it may feel wispy and easily forgotten. This is how thought is often considered, and we would like this book to help people understand thought in a different way.

Thought is actually elastic and concrete at the same time. It does not just run through your mind and then disappear into nothingness. It has an energy and a shape and an intention and an effect—every single one of those many thoughts that goes through your head each day. Part of our working with you and with every person is to help you shape those thoughts, to control what goes through your mind, to practice discipline.

Think, for example, of an attitude of victimhood. It is a feeling that you are not in control of life, is it not? And that means you are not in control of your thoughts, which is how you perceive life. The more you can anchor your thoughts to something real, which is love, the more strength you will have as the foundation of every structure you build while you are here. Does that make sense?

This is why you can literally think of loving thoughts as the building blocks for everything you achieve and create in your life. It is the loving thoughts that provide that bedrock. And to the extent that you can train your mind to believe and extend those loving thoughts, the higher a building you can build. The stronger a struc-

"

Loving thoughts are the building blocks for everything you achieve and create in your life.

"

ture you will have. The more unshakeable it (and you) will be. The more impact it will have. Whether it's the tallest building doesn't matter. It's the strength of what you create in you that people will feel and be inspired and comforted by. This is what reminds people of who they are.

Understand the word "cause."

The word "cause" comes from a root that means "to do." It certainly means having an impact on something else, yet this is not what I want to discuss. Instead, I want you to think of the word "cause" as "influence." It is not an all-or-nothing "this causes that." Stress doesn't cause cancer. Chocolate doesn't cause pimples. Fear doesn't cause war. All of those things have an influence on the outcome, but they are not the single and only cause. There are other factors at work in everything, and this is what your readers need to remember.

Saying that something is a cause is actually rather a limited statement, even though finding causes for conditions or outcomes in your world often signals a great advancement in research. For instance, when it was found that penicillin caused infection to be healed, that was a leap forward in human understanding of healing. But to say that penicillin is the only cause of healing would be limited in scope and understanding.

There are always other forces at work in everything you do in your world, and we are a vital part of that. I don't say this to toot our own horn, as you say, but to point out that assigning cause only to the physical negates a wide and deep reservoir of assistance that you can draw on more easily if you know that it's there.

For instance, let's say you have a child with autism and you want to find the cause. Was it a vaccine that caused it? A genetic code? Hormones in the child's diet? One or more of these might have contributed or influenced the child, but there is a spiritual basis for the condition as well. If you are so focused on finding the cause that you miss the spiritual aspect, then you are missing the miracle.

You cannot be part of a world community that includes the non-physical world as well and ignore the impact of our energy on your planet, just as you cannot put money in the bank and expect a return on it without a savings plan. There is a bigger picture here. And often the word "cause" is associated with blame. What causes Alzheimer's? What causes disease? What causes aging? In every case, there is an assumption that the outcome is bad, and that something or someone is to blame.

How would your world change if you accepted instead? Accepted that Alzheimer's is currently a part of the experience in your world, and that there may be meaning in it beyond simply looking for the cause? Maybe, in fact, we could help you alleviate the symptoms and the disease altogether.

"

If you are so focused on finding the cause that you miss the spiritual aspect, then you are missing the miracle.

"

It is important to remember that nothing is a punishment. No one is being punished. Nothing is broken. But your expectations that everything will happen in your way along a certain and specific thread can make it very difficult for us to help you.

This is important to emphasize in the book because when we say your job is joy, it does not mean that you are guaranteed a life without hardship or struggle. Hardship and struggle are not necessary and will fade away the more you see through them to our world. But they will not be eradicated from your life overnight, nor would you want them to be. The greatest hardships often yield (cause, if you will) the greatest growth, even though growth can be achieved in other ways.

What no one knows is why things happen. The things that happen in your daily life are the amalgamation of more factors than you can fathom—of contracts and intentions made before you were born, of energy patterns in any particular moment in the cosmos, of situations in your parents' lives while you were in the womb, of events in opposite parts of the planet among people you will never meet. Trying to look for the cause of everything can lead you down a very narrow and lonely path, because your companion along the way may very well be the ego saying, "Why? Why is life so hard?"

Life is not hard when you accept that it is multidimensional—that it includes autism and Alzheimer's, flunking tests and subway accidents. Look to us for understanding and let us help you with the changes you can make to grow and heal yourself and others. When you see life as this rather than as a guarantee of entitlement, you will have a different and more joyful experience. Embrace it all. We are here with you always.

Live worry free.

❥ Where we are, of course, there is no worry. There is trust, there is knowledge that all is well, there is peace and contentment. How can that be? Because we know that all our needs are taken care of. We have the ultimate sense of security. Our well-being is not defined by money. We do not develop physical ailments. We are not limited by any beliefs. And so the whole concept of worry is foreign to our territory, although we are very much aware of how it affects all of you on the physical plane.

The question, then, is how can you experience more of what we experience, even while you're in a body? Because, as you know, what we're experiencing is reality, and the worry you're experiencing is not.

Here is what we advise (this also works to build your relationship with us). Sit quietly each day for five minutes and imagine that you are where we are. Imagine that you are in the nonphysical form. This may be difficult for people at first, but with practice it will become easier, and certainly a welcome part of their day. This is what you often do during your dreams. You escape the physical and return to the nonphysical, which is why the limits of time and space don't apply in your dreams and things can seem so nonsensical.

In your daydreams, the point is not to achieve the nonsensical, but merely the nonphysical. Allow yourself to feel what it's like to be transported without a body as your vehicle. Imagine what it feels like to never experience a sneeze or a cough or a dread of cancer. Experience what it feels like to know that there are no money problems because money is not needed. Everything you want already exists and is available to you simply by thinking about it, so there is no currency except your own focused thoughts.

Imagine feeling what it's like to spend "time" doing whatever occurs to you in the moment and feeling no sense of irresponsibility or fear that you're not doing what you're supposed to do, that you're not being productive. Imagine having vast libraries of knowledge available to you that you can visit at any time. Imagine that you are surrounded by people who love you and who you know in the closest ways so that loneliness is an impossibility. Imagine being able to soar and fly and jump and leap and whiz around without limitations. Imagine not harboring blame or judgment or anger toward anyone, including yourself, because there is nothing to be angry about since fear is nonexistent.

Imagine all these things daily, allowing yourself to fully feel the emotions and sensations of all these things not just in your body,

"

Imagine not harboring blame or judgment or anger toward anyone, including yourself,

"

but in your mind. You will be willingly triggering the higher Self part of your mind, engaging the memories of your time here, which you've had repeatedly.

You may experience a sense of coming home, of being at ease and surrounded by light and color. What you experience will be unique to you, but by repeating this activity for many days, you will be up-lifting your higher Self mind and quieting the fear-based ego mind. And that will help you a great deal with worry. Over time you will be much less reactive to worry because you will default to a feeling in which worry is not possible. The feeling of worry will become for-eign to you, and the feeling of all is well will become a norm.

Do this daily. It is the easiest thing in the world. The ego will try to stop you. But do it anyway. Fully enjoy it. It will change your life. We will help you.

Know that you are creative.

Creativity is not just a talent some people have. It is the intentional partnership between our world and yours, brought into human form by your willingness to listen.

Creativity shows in so many different ways that you're not aware of. If you love to decorate your home, this is creativity. If you know how to make an app, this is creativity. These things will be easier and more fun for you the more you work in collaboration with us.

There is no problem you can't solve. This is the resourcefulness and resilience of human beings. It's not that some people have it and others don't. It's that the ones who seem to have it are listening in some way more carefully and have not given up hope because they know there is something else that sustains them.

You are creativity. You are literally a creative thought. Listen to us about how to use that creativity, and you will find life flows much more easily and happily. You don't have to have problems. You think of creativity as creative problem solving, but there is no problem to be solved except by your own imaginings. You create a problem, then you create a solution.

What if you didn't have the problem in the first place? What if you trusted that all is well because you will always, with our help, find a solution to whatever challenge or opportunity comes along? And you get to do this without bitterness or angst. Simply asking, listening, implementing. It really is that easy.

Know that we are not withholding things from you if they do not manifest as quickly as you like or on your schedule. There are always reasons for the timing. Some of them we can express and explain to you, and others will never be known to you while you're in physical form. Trust. Trust, trust, trust. We can't stress that enough.

You try to make things so hard by setting plans and then worrying about how they'll unfold and evaluating whether everything is working out right and wondering what will happen next and judg-

"

We will say it over and over: this life does not have to be hard. Trust us to give you what you need when you need it, and we will.

"

ing what happened before. It's exhausting, and while we are not easily exhausted, you are, and we want to help you move out of that pattern of fear and into a pattern of love. Simplicity. Ease. Acceptance.

We will say it over and over: this life does not have to be hard. Trust us to give you what you need when you need it, and we will.

You needn't expend all the energy checking in every five seconds to see if we've done it yet.

Understand "allowing" and "accepting."

People use the words "allowing" and "controlling," but there is better terminology. Think of it this way: if you are allowing someone to do something, there's a judgment involved. You are giving them permission to do it; you are the gatekeeper. You control whether the faucet is on or off to allow water to flow. Allowing and controlling are actually the same thing.

Accepting, though, is an awareness that there is no gate or faucet. There is simply a flow, and you can accept it or not. So, let's talk about accepting. When you accept the universe's abundance and joy to fill you and permeate every cell of your being, which is your true state, you are experiencing the kingdom of heaven, which is all there is. It is not a destination that you earn or struggle your way to find. It is simply an acceptance of Truth into your life.

That is why partnering with Spirit creates a life of peace and purpose, because you need us to remind you of this. We won't nag you. But we will nudge you to wake up and remember. Remember that it doesn't have to be hard. Remember that you don't have to be angry. Remember that you needn't be disappointed. Remember that life can be good and abundant. Remember that even when life seems difficult, we are here to comfort and guide you. Remember that you're never alone. Remember that when you start to control and allow, we are here reminding you to simply accept.

Many people will scoff at the idea of ease in life. But this is the ego talking. Do you think life is hard in the kingdom of heaven? Do you think we want you to experience strife and hell while you're here? That is not your inheritance. It is not necessary. There can be growth in it. But there can be growth without it, too. What growth do you want? Growth leads to happiness. Why not just be happy now? Why do you make it a destination when it's available to you in this very second?

We want you to wake up and move forward with pleasure and clarity. We know this will not always be the case. But with our help, you can experience this more than you might ever have dreamed. You can experience the tribulations from a different place where you don't feel surrounded and held hostage by them. You don't have to be inside them. You can be outside, witnessing, noticing, learning, and still remembering the peace and joy that are yours always.

196

Work with us. We have so much to teach you and so many ways to help you. If you feel obstinate or suspicious or cynical or skeptical or petulant, so what? We are still here. We are here with you always, and we will always help you, in every single moment, move from fear to love. Sit quietly, take a deep breath, ask, and take our hands.

Final Tips

We've covered a lot of ground in this book, and it's still just a speck in terms of everything we could discuss about collaborating with Spirit. As you begin tuning your ear to the voice within, there are several ideas that deserve to be underscored.

So, finally, here are key points to remember as you co-create with your guides.

Don't engage in spirit envy.

"Well, she can *see* her guides and I can't, so I must be doing something wrong." This is a common stumbling block, and it's all the work of the ego, which wants to turn even spiritual growth into a competition.

"

*We have free will,
and your spiritual
guidance cannot
violate that.*

"

You will experience your spiritual guidance in a way that serves a particular purpose—a purpose you'll understand as the relationship grows. For instance, I've been frustrated in the past that I can't see my guides clearly and consistently like some people do. But when I asked them about it, they were very clear: if I could see them, I wouldn't listen as well. And for me, because I have to listen deeply to hear the guides, I've become better at listening to other people deeply. That's one of the things I'm supposed to do, and the way in which I work with my guides makes me better at it every day.

There is no right or better way to build your relationship. No matter how you do it—through listening, seeing, feeling, writing, drawing—you'll be relying on more than your five senses. In the end, you'll have a *knowing* that's beyond anything you can touch, taste, hear, see, or smell.

Know that the form of your communication may change and evolve over time.

From childhood to adulthood, you make new and different friends. You seek out different advisors. You move from one job to another as your interests and expertise evolve.

This is true with spiritual guidance, too. One day when my niece was visiting, we sat at the dining room table for hours and had a deep, heartfelt talk about what lay ahead in life for both of us. As I said goodbye to her that day, I could feel something imperceptible shifting.

When I went to bed that night, I asked what happened, and I heard that my guides had changed, much like the changing of the guard at Buckingham Palace. I was surprised—shocked, actually. I hadn't been aware of something like this before.

As I focused to meet my new guides, I saw camouflage military uniforms. This surprised me, too. "You have a big mountain to climb," they said, "and we're here to get you to the top safely." Over the next couple of years, they did.

As your vibration rises throughout your life, you'll need guides at different energy levels. Build the relationship, and know that it will change.

Remember that guides can't intervene unless we ask for help.

Underline this, put a big star by it, cut it out, and put it next to your computer.

You have free will, and your spiritual guidance cannot violate that.

As always, we can understand this best by examining parallels in our human existence. For instance, your teenager

"

*I've come too far
to take orders from
other people's egos.*

"

daughter is asserting her independence and making questionable choices. You want to help, but you know the best thing is to stand by and watch her make mistakes. You want to reach out and catch her when she starts to topple, but you know that the mistakes will be valuable lessons if she chooses to learn from them. Then one day she asks you for help, and you're *right* there without judgment or "I told you so."

No matter what happens in your world, you'll find peace and purpose faster if you ask your guides for help, along with a simple question: "How can I use this situation to grow?"

Honor the paths of others.

Know that just as you have your own path, so does every other person on the planet. This includes your children, your grandchildren, your spouse, your neighbors, your business partner, and your best friend. As much as your ego would like to control what they do and shape their lives in the way that you think is best, their life is truly between them, God, and *their* guides.

Your job is to see the light in them, support them, teach them, and guide them with love and kindness and forgiveness. But also to trust that the decisions they make and the paths they follow, which may seem wrong or heedless to you,

"

*No matter
what happens in your
world, you'll find
peace and purpose
faster if you ask your
guides for help.*

"

will serve their soul in a way you cannot understand. When your fears about them come up, send them light and love, and ask for *your* fear-based thoughts to be healed. Then trust that their relationship with their guides will grow and flourish, leading to soul growth beyond your ability to measure.

Release any expectations about timing.

Know that the help you need will show up when you need it, and often not a minute before. I learned this early with my Jolly Green Giant slippers, and I continue to learn it. I've talked with my guides about it. "Really," I say, "do you have to wait until the *very* last minute?" The answer typically is yes, although I've found that the more I trust my guidance, the more I surrender control, knowing the cavalry will always ride in at the perfect time.

Don't let others' egos direct your life.

When someone tells you to hurry, it might be time to slow down. When someone says speak up, it might be time to be quiet. Be a rebel in your own way—not to create conflict, but to be true to yourself.

We often create drama because we're mad at ourselves for not being who we are. By following your guidance, you'll

"

*Know that
the help you need
will show up when you
need it, and often not
a minute before.*

"

alleviate the need for chaos, and you'll become impervious to demands that come from the fears of the outside world.

To remind yourself, write this down and put it next to your computer:

"I've come too far to take orders from other people's egos."

Let go of expectations about your life.

The ego believes life should look a certain way or follow a prescribed trajectory. Get a certain job. Make a certain amount of money. Stay where you're comfortable.

That's why midlife crises occur: you wake up one day and realize you're living the life that the world expected of you, but it doesn't have anything to do with *you*.

In our women's spirituality program a few years ago, one woman described her crisis this way: She'd raised her children into adulthood—thirty years of parenting and taking care of their needs. When they were all out of the house and settled, she decided to go back to school. On the first day, she went through the cafeteria line at lunch. On the dessert table was a bowl of chocolate pudding, prompting her to ask a life-changing question: "Do I *like* chocolate pudding?" She realized that, after all those years of taking care of others' needs, she'd forgotten what *she* liked, what *she* wanted. That began a deeper and more intentional building of her own life, with Spirit's help.

By opening yourself up to co-creation on the level of Spirit, you'll experience life on your terms. It will be scripted and designed specifically for you. And it will most likely be an adventure beyond what you ever dreamed.

Know that what other people think of you is none of your business.

That's one of my favorite quotes, and it's worth repeating. We all have people in our lives who will scoff at the very mention of "spirit guides." But they can be our greatest gifts. Use their doubt to bolster your resolve.

Work with your guides to co-create the life that's right for you, despite any naysayers in your world. Know that, once you're no longer judging yourself for talking to Spirit, others won't judge you either.

Remember that the willingness to believe makes all the difference.

The power of belief makes anything possible. A friend demonstrated it a few months ago when she got a job she'd been focused on for two years. It offered her the hours and lifestyle

"

*The power
of belief makes
anything possible.*

"

she wanted. So even though she didn't have seniority and wasn't sure the job would ever come open, she worked with her spirit guides to keep her eyes on the goal. Sure enough, in a chain of events she could never have choreographed, the job opened up at the perfect moment, and it was hers.

Sometimes, of course, life takes a much more difficult turn. Loved ones die, companies lay off workers, children go down arduous paths. But belief holds out the promise that the world will right itself again, and that no event, no matter how devastating, can permanently silence joy.

Asking with faith, trusting in possibilities, and taking the necessary steps—they all allow us to make our desires real. Not just because special gifts are bestowed on us at random, but because Spirit is right here with us, ready to support us.

If complete faith isn't possible right now, that's fine. It all starts with a *willingness* to believe.

Believe that what you want is what you can have. Believe that this is an abundant world. Believe that as you state your intentions, focus on them, ask for help from Spirit, and take right action, you are reeling in your desires like you've cast your invisible fishing line in abundant waters.

These are my wishes for you: That your thoughts dwell on the beauty of this miraculous world. That you live the life of the mystic, guided and comforted by Spirit. And that, like my Jolly Green Giant slippers all those years ago, your desires arrive by the power of your belief.

And, finally, Ella gets the last word.

🐦 When you are looking to anyone outside yourself for answers, remember that while physical friends can help you, your greatest and truest help will be what comes from inside you, from your inner guidance. The ego wants you to give away your power to others and turn to someone else to heal or direct you. But you have the ability to heal. You have everything you need to create and love and heal. You are always the expert of your own life when you co-create with your guides.

Start training yourself to turn inward rather than outward when you are feeling troubled or alone. This is not to say that people in your life can't also support and guide you. You will find that, while your guidance is strong and sure, you will still doubt it and yourself, and you'll need to hear the affirmations from people around you as well.

But the point of co-creating your life with Spirit is that you create the life that is your unique fingerprint. There are no cookie cutter souls. There need not be any cookie cutter lives. Ask your guidance where you are limiting yourself by other people's notions of who and what you should be. Ask your guidance to help you release those limitations and see yourself in your grandeur instead. Ask your guides to help you have the courage to choose the path that's right for you. Ask your guides to help you trust them and yourself so you can be the greatest expression of love that you came here to be.

Amen. We love you.

And I love you, too. Thank you.

You are most welcome. It is an excellent day.

Acknowledgments

WRITING A BOOK may seem like a solitary act, but more often it's a team effort. That was certainly the case with *Let Your Spirit Guides Speak*, which took shape more effortlessly than I could have imagined thanks to the help of Ella, my writing guide.

Sitting down with her each morning and asking, "What are we writing about today?" turned this book into a daily act of discovery, and it made the summer of writing a time I'll always remember.

In addition, I have many lovely (and incarnated) souls to thank. They include:

My agent, Stephany Evans of FinePrint Literary Management, for becoming a trusted friend and advisor.

My editors, Caroline Pincus and Greg Brandenburgh, for being enthusiastic and steady supporters of the book from the beginning.

The production and design staff at Red Wheel/Weiser for treating this book, as always, with loving hands.

The Common Thread group in Des Moines, Iowa, for inviting me to speak about co-creating with Spirit—a presentation that became the foundation for this book.

My nephew Timothy Landwehr for asking important questions and offering his soul support.

My friend Jude Richardson for reading a late draft of the book and providing thoughtful feedback as I worked on the final revisions.

All the students, clients, and workshop participants I've had the honor to meet and work with over the years. Their willingness to share their stories and explore their own connections to Spirit has been a constant source of joy.

My husband Bob for continuing to be the calm and steady presence I knew from the first time I saw him in my visualization with the Lady in the Blue Dress.

And the Source we all share in this world and the one beyond, connecting us and making all things possible with Love.

About the Author

DEBRA LANDWEHR ENGLE is the author of *The Only Little Prayer You Need: The Shortest Route to a Life of Joy, Abundance, and Peace of Mind* and *Grace from the Garden: Changing the World One Garden at a Time.*

She is the cofounder of a women's program of personal and spiritual growth, teaches classes in *A Course in Miracles,* and offers workshops and presentations worldwide.

Through her company, GoldenTree Communications, Debra helps authors develop and publish their work. In addition, she writes the *Everyday Miracles* blog at *www.patheos.com.*

Debra lives with her husband Bob in Madison County, Iowa, home of the famed covered bridges. You can visit her at *www.debraengle.com.*